Mr Beeton's Book of Household
Mis Management

Mr Beeton's Book of Household ^{Mis} Management

In choosing eggs, apply the tongue to the large end
of the egg, and, if it feels warm, it is new and
may be relied on as a fresh egg.

Mrs Beeton (1836-1865)

Colin Beeton

The Chignal Press

First published in 2008 by The Chignal Press

© 2008 Colin Beeton

The author has asserted his moral right

A catalogue record for this work is available from the
British Library

ISBN 978-0-9559077-0-8

Illustrations © Mike Turner

Printed and bound in England by IntypeLibra, Wimbledon

To: Mary, Clive, Louise, Elizabeth

With acknowledgements and help from
Jackie Voyez and Barbara Inkster
Also Isabella Mary Beeton

Disclaimer

The author of this work has made every effort to ensure information in this book is as accurate as possible. It is not a substitute for specialist or medical advice; knowledge is changing year by year.

The author cannot be held responsible for any errors or omissions or any actions that may be taken by a reader as a result of any reliance on the words contained in the text.

Abbreviations:

Mrs Beeton: Isabella Mary Beeton or Isabella or I.M.B.
F S A: Food Standards Agency

Contents

1

Introduction

When my wife died from cancer I was unprepared for the needs of a beneficial diet. During her life I had enjoyed the fruits of her recipes and cooking. My own subsequent mismanaged efforts towards this branch of living lead to the title of this book. It has been an awakening challenge to leading a healthy life; understanding diet and nutrition is an aim.

Older readers and those living alone may identify with this challenge. I feel that if we tweak the human body enough through diet it should be possible to give support more easily. A brief description of some of my efforts at cooking and managing a meal are included. Experienced cooks will take food preparation in their stride. My early experiences since my wife's death indicated that much time is spent in the planning ahead, buying, recipes, cooking and clearing up later. With a garden to maintain a much restricted social life was indicated. This was not acceptable and I decided to bone up on nutritional benefits of foods that would reduce the time spent in the kitchen.

We now have so many options of what to buy that we need to be careful not to choose unhealthy foods. This is in itself a minefield. It relates to seeking the centre of a maze; hopefully after the cooking and eating then some satisfaction.

I discovered that nutrition is a limitless subject with additional choice each day. It occupies so many 'experts' that we need to tread warily; advice should be taken with a pinch of low sodium salt. For example the supply of organic food is increasing by 10% yearly; then it is reported that some produce has been grown with pesticides. Options from processed foods may include so many additives, E numbers and flavourings that there could be an allergic reaction.

Our education does not emphasize nutrition as a subject; there is more interest in cars than the body and yet both need servicing.

To achieve my objective and to still live within guidelines I have quoted and interpreted from daily news media, magazines, periodicals, books and on-line. I have endeavoured to extract salient parts without misquoting the objectives.

The World Health Organisation in their annual report 2003 referred to the greatest risk factors to health: after tobacco, diet is the greatest single preventable disease of ill health; 60% of world deaths are clearly related to changes in dietary patterns and increased consumption of fatty, sugary and processed food.

Progress in medical science is, optimistically, leading to the prevention of cancer. It is not an unworthy hope, for in Mrs Beeton's day the cause of cholera was just being solved. If we eat and live well with an appropriate diet we should be able to reduce our risk from it; at the same time prevent other chronic diseases. Within the chapters on heart disease, obesity, living longer, recommended foods are often repeated; importantly fruit and vegetables.

I have dwelt on breakfast, including bread and cereals, as an important part of diet; provided we relate to the nutritional information.

A period of eating out and also buying processed foods from supermarkets led me to realise the importance of nutrition. Eating out may be a pleasure but as many food writers and critics so often testify quality may be lacking. Processed foods are no doubt prepared with great skill by chefs; they are making them up to order. They usually contain too much unsuitable flavouring.

Buying from supermarkets is a debatable subject and I have commented upon their selling ploys and marketing policies. They have a grip on many of us and I have described my view of their ways to attract and mislead us. Included are an analysis of some processed foods. I make no apology for dwelling on their power over us for we are told that 80% of what we buy is from their stores.

The role of the Food Standards Agency (FSA) is government backed. Its aim is to protect the public from untoward claims and to give advice. This sounds good but in reality the FSA must find it very difficult to keep up with the developing power of the supermarkets. If we want more local redress we do have Local Authorities with assigned duties we can contact if we are dissatisfied.

I have included a few words about Isabella Beeton's life with her husband Sam. She was well complemented by Sam's publishing experiences. When she died the average age of mortality was in the mid sixties. Average age of death is now 77 for men and 81 for women. Medical science and diet have undoubtedly played their part in extending life. Isabella in her Book of Household Management may well have played a part in this.

It is a saying that we all have a book within us. Those who are living a long life and who are separated or living alone may be interested in my experiences of managing or mismanaging a new lifestyle.

Hopefully you as a reader will pick up a few points to make your life a healthier one.

2

Mrs Beeton and her Book of Household Management

Isabella Mary Beeton burst into mid-Victorian life as a writer on food, recipes and management of a household. Information that she was able to give was a godsend to the growing middle classes. She was an extraordinary and remarkable woman. Her books filled a void for those struggling to look after their growing families, and to manage their households. Over the years we had pored over a few of Mrs Beeton's many and varied editions; the earlier ones contained more than 1600 pages of closely written text.

<hr>

Isabella was born in the City of London in 1836. Her parents were Benjamin and Elizabeth Mayson. Ben died in 1841 and Elizabeth married again in 1843. Each had four children.

Thus they started married life with eight children and proceeded to have thirteen more. Isabella was the eldest daughter. She married Samuel in 1856 at Epsom in Surrey. They had four children two of whom survived their mother who herself died one week after giving birth to a son in 1865.

In 1861 the 'Book of Household Management' (BOHM) was published. It became a great success embracing the whole field of domestic science. It included hints on hiring and managing servants and even information on sanitary, medical and legal memoranda. It included 32 pages on 'The Rearing, Management and Diseases of Infancy and Childhood;' another section on the work of the Doctor including 'How to Bleed'. Sadly even with all the information at her disposal Isabella died early.

The book is thorough in its completeness and knowledge. Later editions after Isabella's death were revised, notably following the availability of electricity, generated on a commercial scale in the early 1880's; they included recipes relating to wines, spirits and liqueurs. However it is also said that Samuel Beeton played down news of her death. After his death many more books were published in her name. Many of these little resembled the original. Each still gave much needed information especially to the poor. The Preface to the First Edition opens by saying 'I must frankly own, that if I had known beforehand that this book would have cost me the labour which it has, I should never have been courageous enough to commence it'. She then remarks 'I have always thought that there is no more fruitful source of family discontent than a housewife's badly cooked dinners and untidy ways'. The arrangement and economy of the kitchen is described as the 'great laboratory'. In all there are some 120 utensils that could be purchased for a good class house with the weights and scales as the most important.

In her preface to the first edition of the BOHM Mrs Beeton acknowledges her indebtedness to many correspondents of the 'Englishwoman's Domestic Magazine' and to many other friends. The first edition published in 1861, was an amalgamation of 24 monthly editions of the magazine. It contained some 4000 recipes to couple with Mrs Beeton's desire to promote efficiency, economy, and well being in the household. She would be flabbergasted now at all the labour saving devices available to aspiring cooks. She would have shuddered at the very mention of processed foods, take aways and junk food; also 150 years later, the vast supermarkets dominating the buying and selling of food; the veering away from home cooking; the general pace of modern life.

———————

It was the custom to include food and other advertisements in Mrs Beeton's books and they very often had different ones as each new edition or print came out. One of the more interesting insertions is for Dr. Ridge's Patent Cooked Food from Ridge's Food Mills in North London. Perhaps they were the forerunner of the present day supermarkets. Dr. Ridge's marketing certified that it contained 'all the essentials of a pure dietary necessary to secure a healthy and natural development of bone and muscle a vital necessity to growing infants'. It showed a picture of an infant with the words 'makes them strong to push along' Whatever was in the patented cooked food the author seemingly had the right medical reasons for its promotion.

Our supermarket marketing personnel would be amused at the exhortation for Lamplughs Pyretic Saline. 'It saved my life for the fever had obtained a strong hold on me. In a few days I was quite well'. It then went on to list the names of eight doctors who gave 'unqualified testimony of the importance of the discovery and the immediate value of THIS GREAT REMEDY.' We can imagine the litigation that these statements would have sparked today. Among the advertisements are those inserted by Huntley & Palmers Limited, Cross & Blackwell Limited, and Oxo cubes – 'focus on flavour'. They are names that have stood the test of time.

Interestingly New Zealand features and their exported lamb would have been popular. One advertisement gives a little history lesson by saying 'when Captain Cook landed in New Zealand on 8 October 1769, he found a land of immense fertility which has developed into a vast treasure house, from which comes huge quantities of the finest lamb for Britain'. For economic reasons their lamb is now mostly exported to far eastern countries.

Later editions included 'Mrs Beeton's Cookery Book.' It was brought out towards the end of the 19th century and it cost only a shilling (5p) because the full edition of the BOHM was too costly. In the preface to a new edition of ' Mrs Beeton's Everyday Cookery' the words 'within the last few years we have been drawn to feel that for all girls in every station of life, cookery should be a necessary part of education.' A prophetic remark for there has been much recent publicity about the standard of food prepared for children's school dinners during their education.

———————

Isabella Mary Beeton's marriage to Samuel was very compatible in every sense of the word and Samuel was a successful publisher. He died 12 years after his wife in 1877, at the age of 46.

There have been several biographies of Mrs Beeton and one that is much more comprehensive than any is 'The Short Life & Long Times of Mrs Beeton' by Kathryn Hughes published in 2005. My judgement about the life of Mrs Beeton needed to be revised after I had read Katherine Hughes' biography. The work she put in to complete it was exhaustive and so well researched that it could be said to be beyond any other conclusions.

———————

This is not, however, to ignore two other biographies written with the permission of the family: 'Mrs Beeton and her husband' by Nancy Spain published in 1948 and 'Mr & Mrs Beeton' by H. Montgomery Hyde published in 1951. Nancy Spain looked admiringly in detail at many of Mrs Beeton's recipes and completion of a work of over half a million words. She refers to the editing and authorship of a girl of 26 who had lots of other things to do. Nancy Spain's biography is witty and very readable. She fails, however, to recognise the importance of Sam Beeton's contribution to the eventual publication of the first Book of Household Management. She quotes a column in the English Women's Domestic Magazine where Samuel seeks the results of their readers' experiences in cooking, pickling, preserving etc. saying that all would be tried and tested 'before publication'. Nancy Spain also says that Isabella skimmed other recipes from current writers for the cream of their recipes which would then be put through her tests for good eating.

———➤•o•⧩———

H. Montgomery Hyde refers to Mrs Beeton's early years when at school in Germany. There she learned to speak French and German fluently; later when preparing her Book of Household Management she was sent a volume of German recipes by her former Headmistress, many of which she used in the BOHM. In addition her friends in France, England, Scotland and Ireland supported her with recipes. Hyde comments on Mrs Beeton's reputation for extravagance by saying that nothing could be further from the truth for her objective in writing was to meet the demand for an economical cookery book. He comments that households of eight or ten children were not uncommon perhaps leading to an impression of extravagance.

———————

I have briefly made references to three of Mrs Beeton's biographies but Kathryn Hughes, besides her own, listed fifteen other writers' interpretations of Mrs Beeton's life.

There are revealing comments in Kathryn Hughes book, when she says, prior to the preparation of the BOHM that Mrs Beeton had a problem 'that Isabella didn't know the first thing about cookery'. The English Women's Domestic Magazine was to form the basis for her recipes in the Book of Household Management and readers responded to requests to send in their own tried and tested recipes. She also received advice from a very experienced cook who had worked in many of the great houses in the country. At that time recipes were not necessarily written down for it was a period of experimenting, testing and tasting food.

Kathryn Hughes refers to the fact that Mrs Beeton 'was a plagiarist who copied other people's recipes; there is no sentence in the Book of Household Management that isn't a tweak or copy of someone else's work'. She pointed out a cookery book by Eliza Acton, whose recipes, were much used.

Other cookery books were being published around this time and I have compared recipes in Eliza Acton's book 'Modern Cookery' published in 1849 (about 680 pages) and

'Domestic Cookery by 'A Lady', believed to be a Mrs Rundell, published in 1821 (about 325 pages). Both are mainly recipes but Mrs Rundell has additional chapters on 'Various Receipts and Directions to Servants'.

I have taken at random, recipes for chicken pie, lemon cheesecake and compared them along with 'Fish'.

Chicken Pie

A Lady (Mrs Rundell) – Cut up two young fowls, season with white pepper, salt, mace and nutmeg, all in the finest powder; likewise a little cayenne.

Eliza Acton – Prepare the fowls as for boiling, cut them down into joints and season them with salt, white pepper and nutmeg, or powdered mace.

Isabella Beeton – Ingredients: 2 small fowls, white pepper and salt to taste, ½ teaspoonful of powdered mace.

Lemon Cheesecake

Eliza Acton acknowledges a Christ-Church-College Receipt.

A Lady (Mrs Rundell) gives two ways of making cheesecake.

Isabella Beeton is quite different and even gives cost of ingredients.

Fish

A Lady – There are over 20 pages of how to choose fish, then with observations on dressing, fish pie, strong gravy and sauces.

Eliza Acton – More limited references to choosing fish but with some 30 pages of various fish recipes.

Isabella Beeton – A comprehensive approach to fish recipes; gives average costs and information on the supply of fish to the London market, noting that 97 million soles and 175 million fresh herrings are delivered each year. In addition there is much information on the National History of Fishes referring to fish eaten in the past around the world. The ancient Romans had a great love of fish; it was very much the food of kings, at least in France and Britain.

No doubt if I extended further into other recipes and headings I would find some evidence of plagiarism; those I have selected appear to have some originality, if only intended to be so.

The book by 'A Lady' contains mostly recipes with some interesting observations on the role of 'The Mistress of a Family' with Parts on 'Cookery for the Sick, and for the Poor' Quite revealing however is the introduction to the book which says 'A collection of nearly Eight Hundred truly valuable Receipts (omitting those in Cookery and Medicine) in various Branches of Domestic Economy, selected from the Works of British and Foreign Writers of unquestionable Experience and Authority, and from the attested Communications of scientific Friends'.

Eliza Acton's book states that it is 'for the use of private families'. It then goes on to say that it is a 'series of receipts, which have been strictly tested, and are given with the most minute exactness'. This is a cookery book which doesn't extend into household management. Nancy Spain makes reference to Miss Acton's English Bread Book from which, she claims, Mrs Beeton took some recipes.

One of the major differences between Mrs Beeton's books and others available at the time was her extensive descriptions; they took into account the rearing of children, medical information and nursing, the responsibilities of domestic servants, the care of children, etiquette at the dining table and housekeeping generally.

————————

There were many other authors of cookery books either before or during Mrs Beeton's life. Two of these were Hannah Glasse and Elizabeth Raffald each of whose recipes, we are told, ended up in the BOHM. It could be the case that each in turn was plagiarised by other contemporary writers. If they were doing the same as Mrs Beeton it would be understandable. Unlike our modern era it was less possible in the mid 1850's to publish comprehensive recipes without back up information and without extracting sufficient from other writers' publications. We should consider that for Mrs Beeton to have borrowed so many recipes it would have been a time consuming exercise; in some cases, as much work as the creation of a recipe; the responsibility for each one was still that of the author.

———➤○ᘿ———

Kathryn Hughes enlarges on the appropriation of recipes by Mrs Beeton in the BOHM: 'The book was both a compilation of recipes and a comprehensive survey of the management of a middle class Victorian household. Management was a very important part of the success of the BOHM.'

Isabella Beeton's additional information over that of Eliza Acton and Mrs Rundell was obtained from Thomas Webster's Encyclopaedia of Domestic Economy published in 1844. This was a vast 1264 page work – 250 pages more than an early edition of the BOHM. In an early preface to the BOHM however there is an admission that chapters relating to household management were 'contributed by gentlemen fully entitled to confidence!' While accepting Kathryn Hughes points, the actual act of putting the BOHM together could have taken up all the working days and years of a short life. There was also the trial and error with recipes, before including them in the BOHM. We should believe Mrs Beeton when she says she experimented with recipes from contributors to the Englishwoman's Domestic Magazine, in her house in Pinner, with the assistance of a servant.

The considerable statistics and explanatory information, after recipes, is not matched in either Mrs Rundell's or Elizabeth Acton's books. This justifying advice shows under headings in the BOHM as, for example, the almond tree, the apple, asparagus, barley, bread, the cabbage, the carrot, celery, parsley, the chestnut. These appear under recipes for soups. Fish are explained likewise. Meat has several pages devoted to it under 'general observations on quadrupeds, sheep and lamb, the common hog and the calf'. There are also separate observations on birds, game, vegetables, puddings, pastry, creams, jellies, soufflés, omelettes and sweet dishes. There follows preserves, confectionery and dessert dishes. She says she 'has endeavoured to make my work something more than a cookery book, and have on the best authority that I could obtain, given an account of the natural history of the animals and vegetables which we use as food.'

Her attention continues on freezing apparatus illustrating 'The Piston Freezing Machine and Ash's Patent Filtering Refrigerator.' After this interlude there is still further consideration given to milk, butter, cheese, eggs, bread, biscuits, cakes and beverages.

My point in scrutinising these general observations is that they could well make up a book in themselves. When we take into account all the work in the preparation of the recipes, and the 'observations', it must have been well nigh impossible in her short life to originate them all. In the Preface to the First Edition Mrs Beeton pays due homage to a 'diligent study of the best modern writers on cookery'.

When referring to meal times Isabella placed an emphasis on a good breakfast as an important beginning to the day for Victorians. In an early edition of her works she listed cold and hot dishes with choices as cold meats, fish, game or poultry, veal and ham pies, game and rump steak pies, ham and tongue as breakfast choices. Hot alternatives were broiled fish, mutton chops and rump steaks, broiled sheep's kidneys, sausages, bacon, eggs, muffins, toast, marmalade, butter. Many of these foods would dismay present day nutritionists for without doubt they would contain excessive fats, sugar and salt – well over the amount per day now recommended.

The main meal of Victorians was dinner but earlier in the day there was the need for food between breakfast and dinner. This depended on the circumstances of the population with the labouring classes probably existing on bread and cheese or bacon, perhaps with some beer. Upper classes would have had more choice with light meals; bearing in mind the main meal of the day ahead. This meal could have been suitably prepared from the vast selection of recipes in Mrs Beeton's books.

Under the responsibilities of 'the Mistress' it is commented that the best articles are the cheapest; it is desirable the mistress should herself purchase all provisions and stores. Experience, she says, will tell her who are the best trades people to deal with. Under the headings of fish, meat, poultry, game are described the proper means of ascertaining their quality. The housekeeper's duties include preserving such fruits as gooseberries, raspberries, strawberries, plums and the making of jams together with the storing of apples. In our world of canned goods, dehydrated foods and freezers we should remember how much more time consuming and complicated it was for Victorian housekeepers to preserve seasonal foods so that there was a good supply for the cold winter ahead. Later editions of the BOHM contain much information on vegetables and fruit. At the end of the century there is a reference to the amount of fruit imported from Canada, Australia, South Africa: also dried fruit and vegetables chiefly from America and Australia.

In early and mid Victorian times it could well have been necessary to shop on foot for purchases from a shop in a main street of a town or village. Individual items would have been bought from different retailers – meat at the local butchers, bread from the bakers, fruit and vegetables from the grocer, fish from the fishmonger. Those days were, however, changing because the industrial revolution was progressing during Mrs Beeton's life: the agrarian economy was being replaced by one dominated by machinery and manufacturing with the first steam trains appearing.

If Mrs Beeton was living today would she have been a Nigella Lawson or Delia Smith? Could she have appeared on TV to demonstrate her recipes to the nation? Perhaps not if we believe Kathryn Hughes. However Mrs Beeton says she spent much time in her kitchen trying out recipes and her evidently strong personality might well have fitted her for such a role. Her book was a best seller so she could have been well marketed and her husband would have made sure such an undertaking was successful.

Could the Victorians have killed themselves with a sur-

feit of fats, sugar and salt in their food. Certainly there is sur-
plus salt in many of Mrs Beeton's recipes. However we are
now advised that our modern food has too much salt, perhaps when we are eating out in a restaurant or fast food
outlet.

—————————

The Times 20 April 2007, Health Editor, Nigel Hawkes, headlined on the front page: 'Scientists prove that a salt diet costs
lives'. He said that the results of a 15 year study offered the
clearest evidence yet that cutting salt consumption saves
lives, by reducing the risks of cardiovascular disease. These
results were first published in the British Medical Journal.

I remember my parents saying that they took me when
young to a Sainsburys store in the High street. In the shop
on either side were counters with assistants at regular inter-
vals in blue and white aprons, taking orders carefully
wrapped in paper for carrying away. At the end of the aisle
there was the Manager keeping an eye on what must have
been a very personal service. This unit is now a Building
Society: a picture hung on the wall for many years; it was
ordered to be taken down because it did not now fit their
image.

—————————

It is very easy to miss some of the pearls of wisdom inserted
in the BOHM by Mrs Beeton which illustrate the all embracing
nature of her work. During her life there were other writers

with their recipes; she gave additional advice on running a home which must have been appreciated by buyers of her book. It distinguishes her from many other writers of her time such as Elizabeth Acton and 'Mrs Rundell'. An example is the two chapters on beverages which include the most popular of the time, together with recipes and much history. Whilst these insertions are unlikely to be original authorships, it does further show the difference in information in the various cookery books of the time. The word 'beverages' does not appear in indexes of Elizabeth Acton, Mrs Rundell's books, or Kathryn Hughes biography.

Books on cookery and household management can reveal much about a period of social history. It is said that with the Boer War and the food shortage of the first and second world wars 'Mrs Beeton' was read as escapist literature; men in Scott's Antarctic Expedition and the prisoners of war in the Singapore prison camps insisted that it was their favourite reading.

In the 1870's the demand for the BOHM continued and was extraordinary; the publishers were always apologising because they were unable to produce enough copies to satisfy public appetite.

Sadly Mrs Beeton did not live to enjoy her success; the fact that her reputation has grown since her death in 1865 could be said to be the result of the playing down of news of her passing particularly by subsequent publishers. Many books bearing her name were brought out after her death.

What we do have is a portrait of the masses and a cameo of life in the Victorian era. It was a key moment in its history. To many people Mrs Beeton is thought of as the writer who 'took a dozen eggs' for a recipe. There were reasons for this because of the large families of the time – Mrs Beeton's mother gave birth to 21 children. Her BOHM is associated by some with an outmoded 'culinary art' – the words Victorians used to describe cooking. It is surprising to see how much of what she set down is useful today. She was aware of the connection between diet and health; advising on management of the household; to the Victorians she became a universal mother, and her book a bible.

"And here, Colin, is one I made earlier."

3

To Cook or Not to Cook

The Rich Fruit Cake

Legend says that King Alfred burnt his cakes. He had a fire, a few pots. I had an oven, gadgets and utensils. I should be able to eat like a king. Christmas was coming and the arrow was directed to the festive iced cake. I intended it to be the centrepiece of the table.

The multi coloured picture of the finished cake in the recipe book looked enticing with its cherries, currants, sultanas and raisins. I just had to follow the recipe. The preparation time was shown as 15 minutes. Several hours later having discovered I did not have the right sized baking tin, and visiting a supermarket to buy 20 ingredients, I was ready, or so I thought.

After spending so much time in preparation I had a slightly sinking feeling that the next stage would not be straightforward. The recommended cooking time was 3½ hours. I finished the cake, decorated and boxed it for the great unveiling one month hence on Christmas day. The accompanied merriment at the time was not entirely attributed to the family festive season.

Helpful comments suggested the cake mix was too moist, more like a plum pudding. I had soaked the dried fruits overnight in fruit juice. I had drained the juice off in the morning but probably insufficiently. The butter and eggs needed to be used at room temperature – not straight from the refrigerator. My cake had sunk. This was because air entrapped when whisking and mixing, should act as a raising agent. The skewer test showed that the cake was not cooked in the middle. It was put back for further baking. I had followed the recommended baking temperatures but not fully allowed for converting them for a fan assisted oven. Greaseproof paper could have been used to cover the cake during baking which allows the cake to cook more slowly. The cake should not, I was further advised, been enclosed in an airtight tin for one month.

The recipe noted that the cake be covered with apricot baking glaze before layering with marzipan. The rollover pack for it was not enough and needed thinning and patching. The rollover icing had the same result. Both folded during the transfer to the cake.

Perhaps I should have used Mrs Beeton's Victorian recipe for a Christmas cake. The main ingredients were given in teacupfuls: 5 of flour, 1 of melted butter, 1 of cream, 1 of treacle, 1 of moist sugar. Other ingredients were 2 eggs, ½ oz (15g) powdered ginger, 8 oz (225g) of raisins, 1 teaspoonful of bicarbonate of soda, 1 tablespoon of vinegar. Mixing was to be thorough with baking in a moderate oven for 1¾ - 2¼ hours. Average cost 1s 6d (7½ p). Her recipe had about half my ingredients with a third less cooking time. She also observes that when cooking we should clear as we go, because muddle makes muddle.

My own efforts were amateurish but it was an interesting experience from which more experienced readers may derive some amusement.

Vegetables and Steaming

All nutritionists acknowledge the benefit we receive from vegetables; this food forms the basis for vegetarian diets along with nuts, pulses, grains and pastas. Vegetables now appear regularly as part of my own diet. This entails quality and buying well in the seasons. Local markets are supported. Significant amounts of vegetables, and fruit, are imported. They face deterioration through storage and the long journeys to their destination.

The value from steaming is acknowledged. Vegetables retain more water soluble vitamins which are lost in boiling because there is a greater loss of nutrients by leaching. A tiered steamer is practical equipment. Food cooked by steaming needs little attention. This can go too far: a burnt base pan is evidence of my mismanagement.

Steaming times for over 20-30 different vegetables are listed in recipe books. These range from five minutes for mushrooms, spinach, mangetout and sliced courgettes to up to 45 minutes for artichokes and swedes. It is one aspect of cooking that is worth the time expended.

"Alas poor christmas cake, I thought I baked you well!"

Pros and Cons

There are too many recipes which assume we have a basic knowledge of cooking techniques. There are thousands to choose from those published each year. The choice is overwhelming.

The present generation has grown up alongside a revolution in processing and cooking. Nutrition and ingredients have been engineered by the supermarket chains. Their printing on food labels is sometimes difficult to read and confusing. We are in an era of ready made foods. Apart from the counters of processed foods we have cake mixes, pastry, fruit pie fillings, custards, sauces.

Storage space for food and equipment is very often not sufficient in modern housing design. It can be a handicap when commencing recipes requiring many ingredients. There is invariably a lack of space in sheltered housing for the elderly.

Supermarkets do not seem interested in single buyers who are often faced with packaged foods for two to four persons. Many published recipes are for four to six. Mrs Beeton's average five to six persons but increase for family dining.

I have followed selected recipes to experiment with cooking. Numbers of ingredients and stages are given with notes on the results.

Recipe	Ingredients	Stages	Notes
Potato & leek soup	8	10	Vegetable dish for regular meals – nutritious and worth repeating
Apple & blackberry crumble	3	6	Ready made crumble made a quick dessert
Shepherds pie	7	10	Mince underdone – more potato needed
Cheesecake	11	8	Digestive biscuit base not right. Topping tasty but too much fat and sugar
Quiche	12	7	Ready made pastry benefited from longer cooking time than listing. Fairly tasteless with too much milk

Recipe	Ingredients	Stages	Notes
Carrot cake	9	6	Telephone call while cooking and overcooked. It was moist and decided not to ice.
Fish pie with sauce	11	9	Longest cooking time. Four saucepans used and muddled through. Surprisingly eatable result
Fruit pie	2	4	Ready made short crust pastry and fruit pie filling – quickest, easiest, pastry needed more cooking time

While being able to control salt content, there was too much saturated fat and sugar in the dessert dishes. The amounts are significant. It leads me to comment further upon them in later chapters and to investigate associated diseases.

I recognise my limitations in the kitchen and conclude that cooking takes too much time. For the future I have decided to cook as little as possible. If I eat the right dietary snacks it should lead to nutritional and ingredient gains with the benefits of fruit and steamed vegetables.

Occasional eating out will also play its part; it gives greater social contact for the single older person.

4

Breakfasts – Eat like a King

Waking up may be hard to do. We have been fasting for hours. We need to replenish the body; not rush out after a cup of coffee; both adults and children may be nodding off by mid-day. Perhaps we should follow the old saying of breakfast like a king, lunch like a prince, and dine like a pauper.

———⊳●⊲———

Marketing slogans and advice tell us that breakfasts give a good start to the day, because of their nutritional benefits and ingredients containing minerals and vitamins. Scrutiny is needed; we may be running into a trap because of another dose of salt, fat and sugar. Some of Kelloggs enticements are laughable: 'its ludicrously tasty (crunchy)' 'your spoon cannot escape the fruit (Fruit and Fibre)' and 'see if you can feel great in a fortnight (All Bran)'. These are accompanied by strong visual images markedly aimed at children. Too often this marketing is meaningless and misleading. Kelloggs marketing has changed, becoming more down to earth when they say 'wake up to breakfast' or 'people who eat breakfast every morning tend to perform better during the day.'

However, Kelloggs have a confusing array of brands including for example, chocolate wheats, just right, bran flakes, crunch nut, crunchy nut clusters, frosted wheats, raisin wheats, whole grain raisin wheats, Special K. There are the varying package weights and prices to consider with any benefits after reading the nutritional information and ingredients list.

———————

'The Grocer' 20 January 2007 (p.43-51): Helen Gregory revealed the results of a survey of the cereal market. It incorporated research from manufacturers and suppliers. It declared that 'the cereal market is growing at 3.4% year on year. The ready to eat cereals dominate as the biggest category consumed; toast is second with a 28 per cent share. Now cereal bars are the fastest growing at 11 per cent per year.' The research also said: 'wholegrain and multigrain are being touted as key health drivers with wholegrain appealing more to older consumers due to the type of benefit it brings. Prebiotics, fibre and superfoods, as also fruits and seeds, are now a feature of many cereals'.

———————

The benefit to children of a good breakfast presents a challenge to manufacturers. 'The Grocer' remarks 'recipes are changing – as are marketing tactics – to ensure parents are happy with the food their children are starting the day.' It also quoted Which?'s Cereal Reoffenders report; 'it criticised more than three-quarters of the 275 cereals tested for having high levels of sugar, a fifth for high salt and 7% for high levels of saturated fat.' It noted that there are manufacturers working hard to remedy the situation following constant reminders from the medical profession and nutritionists.

An advertisement prepared by Kelloggs was featured in 'The Grocer' on 21 August 2004. It was Kellogg's forthcoming national breakfast week, intriguingly marketed as 'helping mums beat the rush hour'. The company's strategy aimed to 'deliver nutrition, fun, taste and convenience . . . reinforcing the health benefits of breakfast.'

Nutritional information on the packets at Sainsburys showed sugar, fat and salt per 100g in 2004 with figures in brackets for 2007, with some not now on the shelves.

Packet	Sugar	Fat	Salt
Sugar frosted toasted rice cereal	40	0.7	1
Coco Pops	39 (36)	2.5 (3)	1.13 (1.1)
Sugar frosted flakes of Corn (Frosties)	38 (37)	0.5 (0.6)	1.5 (1.1)
Rice crispies Muddles	20	3.5	0.38
Honey Loops	35	6	1.36
Corn Flakes	8 (8)	0.9 (0.9)	2.37 (1.8)
Rice crispies	10 (10)	1 (1)	1.5 (1.6)

Tesco's own brands in 2004 are listed for a comparison with 2007 in brackets – per 100g

Packet	Sugar	Fat	Salt
Frosted flakes	38.1 (38.1)	0.5 (0.8)	1.5 (1.5)
Kids Choco flakes	36.9 –	0.7 –	1.5 –
Kids Choco snaps	38.4 (38.4)	2.4 (2.4)	1.25 (1.0)
Kids Breakfast Boulders	31.1 (29.5)	1.4 (1.3)	1.25 (0.7)
Kids Rice Snaps	9.8 (9.7)	1.3 (1.3)	2.25 (1.5)
Corn Flakes	9.0 (8.9)	0.7 (1.2)	2.25 (1.5)

For both Kelloggs and Tesco there is some reduction in salt content but it should be less; very little effort has been made to reduce sugar and fat content. The nutritional information inevitably requires a knowledge of chemistry with varied listings as thiamine (B1) Riboflavin (B2), niacin, pantothenic acid.

Assuming average levels of sugar in other meals in a day, there is too much in the majority of cereals. If Tesco's nutritional information is typical also of other major retailers own brands they should not be supporting health claims.

Daily Mail 17 August, 2004, Angela Dowden: a week previously The Danish Veterinary and Food Administration rejected an application from Kelloggs to market its fortified cereals: it was on the grounds that the increased levels of vitamins and minerals might be unsafe.

The application was rejected because the iron, calcium, vitamin, B6 and folic acid in Kelloggs cereals and cereal bars are high enough; in some cases a potential health risk when combined with the rest of our diet.

———————

Muesli, as marketed, usually consists of seeds, nuts, dried fruit and fibre; it should be a nutritious bowl to start the day. We may be attracted by the words protein rich, mineral rich, immune boosting or complex carbohydrates as part of healthy eating claims.

Some suppliers do not use the word muesli to describe contents. Dorset Cereals supply a mixture with a blend of 'super cranberry, cherry and almond.' Nutritional information per 100g: sugar 31.4g, fat 7.9g. Sugar is double FSA guidelines. The heading is misleading; cranberries and almonds are only about 8.5% of the contents and cherries 1%. Nuts are a good source of unsaturated fats and out of the total fat of 7.9g, 6.9g is unsaturated.

There is evidence that other 'mueslis' are passed off as good for us. They are high in fat and sugar. There is also natural sugar in fruit to consider if there is lots of fruit. With the misleading marketing and high prices we should select our own ingredients. Suggested are: a base of organic jumbo oats or millet flakes, a selection of dried fruits with some stem ginger, nuts and seeds, brewers yeast, yoghurt. This muesli does not have the flavour of most for it lacks sugar, fat and salt. The dried fruits will have a natural sugar content but dependent on the amount there will be a temptation to add sugar. Potential dental decay from sugar is reduced by the presence of milk. As an alternative to muesli, especially in winter, a bowl of whole grain porridge oats is nutritious; its slow burning energy release has a health gain for the heart. Dried fruits and honey may be added.

Many breakfasts when too high in sugar and salt are part of a poor diet leading to both present and future obesity problems; indirectly other serious diseases. Some cereals come out well, within guidelines, as do wholegrains Weetabix and Shredded Wheat.

It can be an unprofitable chore going through cereal labels to find those high in nutrients, as fibre and wholegrains; lowest in fat and sugar. Most children will not be interested and given the option may prefer a fast food outlet.

We must conclude that the traditional family breakfast is moving to foods that can be eaten on the move while still able to eat 'breakfast' These could include cereal bars, yoghurt, drinks and smoothies. Microwavable products also can provide a quick answer. Porridge used to have an old fashioned image but emphasis is now put on oats in a diet. If we were to stick to a set variety of food this could be boring. A change to a full English cooked breakfast perhaps with an egg would surely not allow us to be accused of overeating. On the other hand if we follow Mrs Beeton's recipes we shall have more than enough with too many calories.

Sugar fat and salt rear their ugly head in another chapter; we just cannot get away from their danger to us. The omission of sugar altogether from cereals would not be acceptable to those who enjoy its flavour.

If there are too many calories we do not exclude them by missing breakfast. A balanced breakfast will surely lead to a healthier lifestyle. It has proven benefits, with weight control, improved concentration, mood and energy.

"Enjoy a balanced diet."

5

Bread – The Staff of Life

Writers of articles on bread suppliers have sometimes tended to make pointed and detrimental comments about the staple food which can form a large part of our diet.

Wheat is grown all over the world; it is milled and ground into flour. The resultant outcome in Britain may not give the same benefits as some comparable countries in Europe; bread is put on a higher pedestal there as part of the necessity of life.

Felicity Lawrence in her book 'Not on the Label'* reserves a whole chapter for 'Bread' (p.102). She describes the happy ritual of buying bread from a local shop and the dough that has taken time to ferment. 'She kneads it gently with her knuckles, folds it to pull it back, pushes it away and gives it a quick roll with the heel of her hand'. The only ingredients required are flour, yeast and water, well made with vital nutrients we need for good health. It was called the staff of life. She says that if the staple of the diet is healthy, then it is much easier to ensure that the diet overall is healthy; the nutritional gulf between a well made wholemeal loaf and a white sliced factory one is enormous.

In criticizing what we see on supermarket shelves, she declares the vast majority of the breads on offer have emerged from the same factories and been made by one industrial method. The baking industry reckons that half of the big retailers' in-store bakeries are using 'pre-baked' dough. Nearly all the remaining in-store bakeries make their bread on the 'premises' with flour, yeast, fat and improvers already measured out by a factory. An improver or 'flour treatment agent' is the logical way to add fats needed in an industrialised process. Packaged bread from a supermarket may list flour treatment agents or be related to E300 recognised as having a function as vitamin 'C'. Emulsifiers E471, E475 and E476 are also used.

⸺⸺⸺

During visits to supermarkets in 2005 I noted other 'E' numbers listed as E472(e) and E481. Examples are 'Hovis White Crusty' and their 'Square extra thick square' together with 'Kingsmill Soft White' and 'Medium 7 day fresh'. Other manufacturers may well include these E numbers and not list them. They are all additives; advice maintains that these are all safe when used in bread.

⟶•⟵

A spokesman for the Food Commission, an independent watchdog, has maintained 'The majority of additives are unnecessary from a nutritional point of view – they are there to make food more colourful or change the flavour'. It noted also that many of the additives are outlawed in other countries including America and Japan as well as leading supermarkets in the UK.

The Food Standards Agency lists 324 'E' numbers of the additives we are most likely to come across on food labels. The subject is a complex one and the FSA states (2007) that official directions for full publication of research may not take place for two years.

On 3 July 2004, Sheila Keating wrote and quoted in The Times Magazine (p.83), from a report called 'Bread Street: the British Baking bloomer?'*. She said that there are over 200 varieties of bread available in the UK and we buy the equivalent of nine million large loaves every day. 80% of them are still the pappy, sliced, wrapped sandwich loaf (75% of which are white). She continued: the big multiples may well have forced traditional bakers from our High Streets but they seem to have replaced them with every permutation from sourdough to soda bread. The majority of in-store breads are 'baked off' from frozen part baked products, or made from premixed packets of ingredients, both including the same litany of improvers.

made from premixed packets of ingredients, both including the same litany of improvers.

I looked at the information on the bread wrapping of the main suppliers and visits were made during September 2005, mainly to Sainsburys and Tescos; breads were selected at random.

Nutrition in grammes per 100g (except calories)	Tesco Value Thick Sliced 800g 25p	Tesco Wholemeal Thick Sliced 800g 43p	Hovis Sunny 800g 75p	Nimble White Sliced 400g 62p
Energy – calories	231 kcal	217 kcal	271 kcal	245 kcal
Protein	8.0	10.3	10.1	9.9
Carbohydrates	46.4	38.4	43.6	46.4
Fat	1.5	2.5	6.2	2.2
Of which Saturates	0.5	0.7	0.6	0.4
Mono unsaturates	0.3	0.8	–	–
Poly unsaturates	0.7	1.0	–	–
Fibre	2.1	6.5	2.4	2.1
Salt	1.0	1.0	1.09	1.38

Nutrition in grammes per 100g (except calories)	Sainsbury's Wholemeal Thick Sliced 43p	Hovis White Granary Multiseed Healthiest ever Hovis £1.04	Kingsmill Gold Moreishly Malted 90p	Kingsmill Soft White Thick 79p
Energy – calories	214	242	232	232
Protein	10.3	10.1	8.7	8.8
Carbohydrates	37.8	41.8	43.1	43.8
Fat	2.4	3.8	2.7	2.4
Saturates	0.4	0.5	0.5	0.4
Mono unsaturates	0.9	–	–	–
Poly unsaturates	1.1	–	–	–
Fibre	7.4	5.7	3.5	2.8
Salt	1.0	1.19	1.22	1.22

Calorific content, which includes starches and sugars, is in the range 214-271 kcal as part of a daily intake of 2000 calories each day. Protein ranges between 8.0 and 10.3g/ 100g. Guidelines indicate that a woman needs 45g and a man 55g each day.

Carbohydrates are listed as 46.4g/l00g for both Tesco value thick sliced and Nimble white sliced. Sainsburys and Tescos wholemeal thick sliced would appear to give the best value. Fat is a rich source of energy but too much can be eaten as part of some breads leading to a need to limit intake. There are benefits from the poly and mono unsaturates to consider and the comparison is confused by their omission from many of the breads listed. Least content of fat is Tescos value thick sliced while Hovis 'Sunny' is quite considerably more.

Generally the wholemeal breads contain more fats than white bread because wholemeal uses the whole of the wheat grain containing the healthy unsaturated fat, and pure white bread is made from the central part of the wheat grain. Fibre content is highest in Tescos and Sainsburys. Salt content is perhaps the most controversial ingredient; the subject of major criticism from health conscious experts. Recommended daily intake is between 5 and 7g/100g a day but has to be taken in the context of other foods consumed in a day. Undoubtedly there is too much salt in all the breads listed. Nimble is the main offender; the total content in most packs exceeds the daily guideline.

We buy bread in supermarkets and the choice can be bewildering. The packaged bread has its nutrition information; that baked on the premises often has none; my request at one major supermarket for its salt content had to be pursued strongly to get an answer. Bread once received a distinctive flavour from the normal fermentation but this is missing. The industrial process has taken over. This involves added salt to give the customer the attractive flavour. Kingsmill say their bread is for a balance of good health and recommends that we increase the amount of bread and other cereals in our daily diet.

Claims from Hovis dwell on their lower salt levels. Their white bread described as 'Hovis lower salt', says 'current dietary advice is that we should aim to reduce the salt in our diets by about one third. This is because salt contains sodium which has been linked with high blood pressure. High blood pressure is a risk factor for heart disease and strokes; cutting down on salt may help to maintain a healthy heart and circulatory system'. Despite this comment, Hovis, as at September 2005, were still selling their other breads with higher salt content. They say their 'Sunny' is their healthiest ever with the addition of sunflower seeds and honey; they refer to lowered salt levels but these are not below some of the other breads I have now listed.

However some other Hovis breads do contain about a third more salt than 'Sunny'. Also the fat levels are more than

Tescos value thick sliced. Hovis have put together a bread named 'Invisible Crust' saying 'no goodness goes to waste' and 'using over 125 years experience we've discovered a way to bake a loaf without the bit you don't like – the crusts'. Perhaps it might have been beneficial to purchasers if Hovis had spent the last 125 years reducing the salt content alone. Nimble have more unusual marketing to attract customers with a sense of humour: 'a moment on the lips – .00000008 of a millimetre on the hips' and 'Diet tip: I only eat chocolate when I'm not looking' Their main serving suggestion is 'eat leaning out of the window so crumbs don't get in bra'. These were on their wholemeal bread, their white bread contained none of these remarks; perhaps the marketing department had been told to calm down when they say 'eating Nimble is being healthy, but no one need ever know' and 'real women love food'. Nevertheless the salt content of their breads is about a third higher than many others. Their packaging is in 400g parcels against other suppliers with 800g; they are more expensive without necessarily giving good value.

———————

Pressure from the media and medical advice has resulted in reductions in salt in bread; the impression received is that the manufacturers have a reluctance to take this action. Perhaps the European Union will do better.

———————

Having digested the nutritional information which manufacturers are required to give, and the consumer to understand, there are lists of ingredients given as improvers. These could be: Alpha_amylse, vinegar, emulsifiers, antifungal sprays, stabilisers, whiteners, added enzymes to make the dough softer and 'improve' the volume and prolong shelf life, vegetable oils and/or vegetable fats, calcium propionate (added to inhibit mould growth), ascorbic acid (Vitamin C), slow treatment agent, acetyltartaricesters of mono-di-glycerides of fatty acids. For a period of 30 minutes on a busy Saturday morning in Sainsburys I did not see one purchaser looking at the information on the packaged bread. Whilst manufacturers are required to state energy, protein, carbohydrate, fat, fibres and sodium (salt) we may be confused when we read the list of ingredients. To understand this is time consuming especially when unusual chemical names are shown.

A visit to Tescos was made on 8 September 2005, when the cheapest Tesco packet of white bread was 25p. At a visit one week earlier it was 19p. It was the figure noted by Felicity Lawrence (p.120) when she said 'In July 2003 the cheapest white sliced bread on sale in the major multiples was 19p.' She continued: 'The cheapest bread is nearly always an own-label loaf, which gives the supermarkets more bargaining power over the suppliers since it undermines the manufacturers own brands by making them look bad value and increases competition between suppliers'. This is a good example of supermarket actions.

————>•◦•<————

Small bakeries find it very difficult to compete. Where any are left in small towns they can be very busy in the mornings and sell out in the afternoons. Fortunately customers are still supportive of their individual baking.

The Sandwich Factory

An earlier edition of Mrs Beeton's Book of Household Management has about 35 recipes for sandwiches. Alphabetically it commences with one named 'Adelaide' made with cooked chicken and ham, white bread with curry butter. The list ends with tomato sandwiches describing what we should do with them: 'pour boiling water over the tomatoes, let them remain immersed for two minutes, then drain and cover with cold water. Allow them to become quite cold, dry well, remove the skins and slice thinly.' Along with creamed butter, white or brown bread, lemon juice or vinegar, salt and pepper, a Victorian sandwich was almost a work of art. All these would have been made at home and they can still be the basis of food for a day out – if we are prepared to give time to their preparation.

We now have many opportunities to buy at supermarkets; additionally at various retail stores, garages, specialist shops in populated cities; also public houses and other 'con-venience' outlets where sandwiches are extra to a main business. The supermarkets in particular, have in the last few years, realised that they are able to make a good return on this product; bread used in the sandwich may come from a 500g packaged loaf on sale in the store for less than 50p. The cost of the bread in the sandwich may average 4p.

Before arriving at the retail outlet, the ready made sand-wiches – the result of factory techniques – will have been refrigerated or chilled and transported to their destination by packaging mainly in sealed plastic containers. They might have been made several days before being placed on the shelves. The refrigeration alone cannot be beneficial to the bread for it creates dampness which surely affects the qual-ity of its constituents. Sandwiches sold may state that they should be eaten within three days. If unsold they may still sit on the shelves to catch the unwary buyer short of time – possibly with a reduced price. They may be tasteless and a dried up or soggy mess by then.

They need to be made attractive to the purchaser, colourings and additives may be included to give the appear-ance of freshness. Above all it can be said that the salt content, so necessary for flavouring and marketing pur-poses, is producing too much salt, as part of the accepted guideline for consumption in one day. Nutritional information is not always listed or it may be shortened. There is a con-siderable license for the retailer. For those pressed for time, and hungry, a sandwich is a quick satisfaction. A buyer may base his purchase on the stated contents. We should consider the visible face of contents thickened at the centre of the sandwich; the spread from this point is seldom the same throughout the sandwich and is deceiving.

The retailer 'Boots' seem to have responded to criticism by marketing sandwiches in malted bread, either in clear plastic with different cut shapes, or packaging in biodegradable material using 'traffic lights' for the constituents. However all that can be seen is its well filled centre through a small circle of clear plastic.

The canteen of a busy major suburban hospital had a line-up of 26 makes of sandwiches in basic white and brown bread priced at between £1.10 and £2.95. They were set in the chilled cabinet in clear plastic with the open side visible. The filling was centred, covering about two thirds of the sandwich. There were two suppliers; one had full nutrition information – the other was abridged. In the nature of a busy hospital at lunch time a name and visible contents alone appeared to be the choice factor. The hospital canteen is a good example of people with limited time requiring a quick meal.

Given a choice perhaps we will make our own sandwiches from one of Mrs Beeton's recipes – if we have time.

* Felicity Lawrence 'Not on the Label' published by Penguin Books 2004.

* Bread Street: The British Baking bloomer? Published by Sustain: the Alliance of Better Food and Farming.

"A healthy one? Er . . . I'll have to ask the manager"

6

Dangers of Salt, Fat and Sugar

Salt

Mrs Beeton refers to common salt as a necessary food 'but the fact is many persons today get too much of it in the form of salt fish and flesh. It is the only mineral habitually added to food as such; the importance of salt as a condiment, as an antiseptic, and an article of food cannot be overestimated. Salt is indispensable, for it makes palatable food that would otherwise be uneatable.' She recommends a day's ration of salt for a healthy man of average size doing moderate work as 1 oz (28g). This is well above that now recommended.

Salt

It is recorded that in Tudor times the upper classes placed the salt container in pride of place on the dining table; it was the first to be set in place after the cloth had been laid. Many recipes listed two teaspoons of salt.

⸺⸱◦⸱⸺

The advice of the Food Standards Agency for October 2004, clarifies the make up of salt. It says that it is made up of two components sodium and chloride. It is the sodium in salt that can lead to health problems. The FSA recommendation for adults is to have no more than about 6 grams of salt per day which means about 2.5g of sodium. Children should have less than this. On average people are actually having 9.5g of salt a day or some 60 per cent more salt than we should. As a general rule they also say that per 100g food, 0.5g sodium is a lot, and 0.1g is a little sodium.

Headlines and comments from the media today bring to consumers' notice the potential health risks from over con- sumption of salt. Daily Mail 17 June 2004 (p.23); Sean Poulter (Consumer Affairs Correspondent) stated that the Government was insisting that salt levels in processed foods must be cut by up to 43 per cent. Daily Mail 14 September 2004 (p.46); Joanna Blytheman, had a banner headline of 'The Great Salt Scandal'. She said that it is a tragic reality of modern Britain that we are killing ourselves with our over consumption of salt thanks to our excessive reliance on

Salt

processed foods. The Sunday Times 4 July 2004 (p.6 News), Jonathan Leake; British consumers eat more salt than most other countries because it is so widely used as a flavour substitute in processed foods.

On 30 January 2006, the Consensus Action on Salt and Health issued a media release relating to their Salt Awareness Week, 2006. It included the aim of preventing salt – related deaths in black people of African or Caribbean descent living in the UK. It explained that they have a higher risk of dying from a stroke than the average population; in many cases these strokes are caused by raised blood pressure resulting from excess salt in their diet.

A banner headline appeared in the Daily Mail 1 May 2007 (p. 49), with an article by Jane Clarke. This headline may confuse because it said 'Too little salt can be bad for you, too'. As a nutritionist she said she had advised a patient who in turn had been told that she had a lack of sodium. The headline needs to be interpreted; while she agrees that health professionals, including nutritionists, are campaigning for greater awareness, with reduction of salt intake, she is saying that too little sodium may affect elderly people on diuretics. These drugs are used for treating heart problems and high blood pressure to reduce excess fluid in the body. As an interpretation of this article the message is more likely to be one of reducing salt intake unless instructed by a doctor.

The Times 20 April 2007, (p.1); Nigel Hawkes, Health Editor, headlined the problem of salt by saying 'Scientists

Salt

prove that a salty diet costs lives,' adding that a 15 year study shows a link to heart disease. Eating less salt reduces the chances of suffering a heart attack or stroke. The findings offered the clearest evidence yet that cutting salt consumption saves lives by reducing the risk of cardiovascular disease.

⎯⎯⎯⎯➤•◦•◀⎯⎯⎯⎯

The Chinese now appear to be taking the dangers of too much salt intake more seriously. Jane Macartney in Beijing writing in The Times, 4 May 2007 (p. 53), remarked that five million small blue plastic spoons are being distributed to households in Beijing, in an attempt to encourage healthier eating. The plan is to get every family to limit its salt intake to only one spoonful a day. There is a message for the rest of the world here for the article goes on to say that the influx of supermarkets in Beijing in the last 20 years, and the rapidly rising affluence in this city, has caused 35 per cent of adults to be overweight. This does not in itself prove that the Chinese eat too much salt but it could well be part of the reason. It is to be hoped that the Chinese will not add the salt to a 'processed' purchase from their supermarkets. Perhaps we should take Chinese research more seriously: we can see that they have not been influenced by Mrs Beeton who often included two teaspoons of salt for an appropriate recipe, as in Tudor times.

⎯⎯⎯⎯➤•◦•◀⎯⎯⎯⎯

Salt

These quotations from the media are only examples of the warnings we are receiving about the dangers of salt in our food. A majority of our salt intake may well come from convenience foods; it is up to us to be more careful which foods we select.

Home cooking is the winner for we should then be able to control our intake – without the proverbial pinch of salt.

Fat

Mrs Beeton in the BOHM is typically direct when referring to fat when she remarks 'whether it be called butter, cream, dripping, meat, bacon, oil or by any other name it is necessary for food, and many are the persons that suffer in health from want of it'. The FSA maintains that we should eat a low fat diet; 'there is substantial evidence that reducing the amount of saturated fat we eat, can lower our chances of developing coronary heart disease. Because cholesterol is closely related to this disease, diets that are high in fat have also been associated with obesity.'

———»•o•«———

We are alerted by headlines from the media:

'High fat found in healthy option food' – The Sunday Times 1 August 2004 (p.4), – Jon Ungoed-Thomas and Nina Goswami.

'Fat-packed lunch. The M&S sandwich that's worst for your waistline' – Daily Mail, 4 October 2004 (p.35).

'Fast food roasted over hidden fats. The Government must act against manufacturers to cut use of artificial fats that are a risk to health'. The Times 7 October , 2004 (p. 30) – Valerie Elliott.

'Fat lot of good? Eating too much white bread may be bad for the waistline' – The Times, 9 July 2004 (p. 10) – Peta Bee

'It must have been something I ate'. The Daily Telegraph

Fat

7 November 2005 (p. 27), – Ian Marber. He suggests that eating the right fats will do our skin more good than costly lotions.

It is in the manufacturers interest to get us to eat more fat because it is tasty, inexpensive and is meant to add to the enjoyment we get from eating it.

———————

The FSA has produced guidelines relating to the terms fat free, low or reduced, in percentage of fats per 100g or 100ml.

> Fat free should be less than 0.15g.
> Saturated fat free should be less than 0.10g.
> Low fat should be less than 3g.
> Low in saturated fat should be less than 1.5g.

For fat to be marketed as reduced it should be lower in fat than other similar ones. It may also claim that it is 90 per cent fat free and therefore of benefit to health. Cakes, crisps and biscuits very often make these claims. Fat reductions do not automatically give benefit. Surveys by consumer groups have discovered that often, when fat levels are lowered, sugar and salt levels rise.

———————

Fat

The FSA suggests cutting down on saturated fats:
> Choose lean cuts of meat and chicken without skin.
> Use semi-skimmed or skimmed milk.
> Cut down on sweets, desserts and chocolates.
> Stick to dry curries, rather than dishes with rich or creamy sauces.

The FSA also relates the process of hydrogenation in the manufacturing process as turning liquid oil into solid fat. During this process a type of trans fat may be formed that raises cholesterol levels in the blood which increases the risk of coronary heart disease. There has been a media campaign against the inclusion of trans fats. It has been recognised by some supermarkets and action has been taken to cut them out.

<hr/>

It is interesting to compare recipes of tomato soups for 1870 and a more modern recipe – both for serving six persons. Mrs Beeton's ingredients are: ¼ lb butter, 1 large onion, 2 or 3 large tomatoes, 2 French rolls, 2 pints of stock, salt and pepper. An average one in 1980 could be: 1 oz butter, 2 large onions, 1 oz plain flour, 2lb tomatoes, 1 pint stock, ¼ pint double cream. Mrs Beeton would always propose the addition of salt for added flavour. Comparatively, fat contents are ¼ lb butter in 1870, and 1oz butter and ¼ pint of double

Fat

cream in 1980; the likely fat content is not much less than in 1870. Salt is not included in the 1980 recipes.

There is an observation by Mrs Beeton under the heading of Margarine. She says that 'margarine is bought by pastry cooks and if well manufactured and sold at a reasonable retail price it would be a most valuable addition to the food of the people who most commonly suffer from a want of fatty food'. We now recognise that fatty food may be destructive to health. Perhaps the Victorians should have had more tomato soup; they would probably have added too much salt.

Sugar

An annual global consumption of sugar of 134 million tonnes carried in 40ft standing trucks would more than encircle the 25,000 miles of the equator. Ingredients lists alone often show how food is overloaded with sugar; it can be addictive.

Mrs Beeton remarks that 'about 1740 it was discovered that many plants of the temperate zone and amongst others the beet, contained it. It was ascertained towards the beginning of the 19th century that sugar exists in the whole of the vegetable kingdom; in the grape, chestnut, potato, but that far above all, the beet contains it in a large proportion. Most of the sugar consumed in England is actually produced from sugar-cane, but of beet-root sugar there is much on the market.'

In August 2004, the Food Standards Agency advised that 10g of sugar per 100g in a day is a lot; in April 2007, they re-phrased this by saying that high is more than 15g sugars per 100g; low is 5g sugars or less per 100g. Should the amount of sugar per 100g be between these figures, then that is a medium level of sugars. They suggest however that we should cut down on foods and drinks that contain lots of added sugar: biscuits, chocolate bars, sweets, jams, fizzy drinks, cola and lemonade. Listed also by the FSA are some foods that we might not expect to have sugar added to them. These are, for example, some breakfast cereals, cereal bars,

Sugar

tinned spaghetti and baked beans. Further advice refers to ingredients; labels should have the biggest ingredients coming first. If sugar comes near the front of the list the food is high in sugar. It also says to watch out for other words which are used to describe added sugar, such as sucrose, fructose, corn syrup and honey.

Supermarkets have often been criticized for the contents of their breakfast cereals; they have contributed towards children's addiction for sugar.

The Times 11 December 2004 'Body & Soul (p. 6), David Rowan commented under the heading 'Sugar is the new threat in the fight against flab – but it is a cunning enemy.' He referred to the Government's White Paper the previous month which called for lower sugar levels in our foods. A more comprehensive survey of sugar was made in the same paper (p. 7-8) by Jane Clarke, under the headline 'The hidden truth – there's more sugar than we think in many everyday products but you can play it safe'. She noted dangers to the body from sugar: consuming too much sugar hinders our ability to burn off fat. Too much sugar can raise levels of certain fatty acids which are linked with high cholesterol. The more often we eat sugary food the more insulin we release to process it. Sugar causes tooth decay. A sweet drink or snack before a meal may make us overeat.

The Sunday Times 6 May 2007 (p.5), Jon Ungoed-Thomas and Mohammed Khan headed an article with the words 'Hello sugar . . . food is getting sweeter'.

Sugar

They pointed out that 'food companies have doubled the amount of sugar they add to some of their most popular products – including soups and cereals – in an attempt to attract sweet-toothed customers'. They compared increased amounts of sugar per 100g in three staple foods between 1978 and 2007. These were Kellogs Special K, Cream of tomato soup and wholemeal bread. Increases varied between 1.6g and 7.4g. Also 'soaring consumption of sugar has been blamed for high levels of tooth decay, and increases in diabetes, with many scientists implicating it in rising rates of obesity'.

The Times repeated the message a day later, with an article (p.11) by Marcus Leroux, under the heading 'Give us this day our daily bread . . . but why put so much sugar in it?'

═══════►◦◄═══════

The comments by those experienced in the food industry generally have increased over the last four years. We are now a nation of sugar junkies. We can assume further emphasis on the dangers of sugar will continue as additional research takes place.

Like tobacco perhaps sugar should have a government health warning.

7

Drinks

A Lifetime of Water

Mrs Beeton says in the Book of Household Management 'to whichever class our beverages belong, water is the basis of them all. Even our solid food contains more water than anything else'. She points out that 'pure water, consisting of two parts hydrogen to one part oxygen does not exist in nature, and when it is obtained by the distillers it is flat and distasteful to those who have not accustomed themselves to its use'. This is used in car batteries. She does not refer to the added taste we get from the earth which makes water palatable. Luckily for Mrs Beeton she lived in the time when the first major filtration plants in the country were installed. One

A Lifetime of Water

of the benefits of these was to reduce the incidence of disease – particularly cholera.

The medical profession advises that we should drink eight glasses of water each day to make about 2 litres. However we should not take this too literally; fluid requirements may be obtained from many sources: fruit, fruit juices, beer, soup, tea and coffee.

———————

If we check out the bottled drinks on the market Mrs Beeton would have been taken aback by some of the contents. Her feelings would have been confirmed if she had heard of the major company 'Coca Cola' who were marketing bottled water in 2004 as 'purified' tap water. It was piped directly from the river Thames in London. It was also alleged that in the manufacturing process it had been contaminated by dangerous chemicals. In the early 1990's 'Perrier' water was analysed and found to contain contamination by benzine; millions of bottles had to be withdrawn from the market. It is also possible that other bottled water for sale is contaminated in some form. It is likely that some of the water Mrs Beeton was drinking was impure. A Water Board official may well be able to prove that their water is healthier than any bottled water other than those from certain natural springs.

The Times 4 June 2007 (Times 2 p.2), quoted the New York Times which one day had devoted 1300 words to the

A Lifetime of Water

fact that many leading American restaurants have banned the type of bottled mineral water whose labels read something like 'flowing from an ancient glacial spring and salted with angels tears' it told customers 'its tap water or nowt'. This commentary would be a good lesson for many British restaurants.

The Milkman

The Sunday Times 30 November 2005 (p.16), Body & Soul, Nick Wyke: 'milk was undergoing something of a renaissance; sales were increasing in 2005 for the first time in 30 years.' he felt this was partly due to the stress being placed on the importance of breakfast together with the branded milks that promise health benefits; the boost from the rise in coffee shops. The passage pointed out the benefits of organic milk reporting that a 'Mintel' survey in 2004, noted an 80% surge in demand. Research showed that organic milk is richer in key vitamins and nutrients than its ordinary counterpart. As a conclusion he said that milk is a vital and cost-friendly part of a balanced diet for any person without lactose-intolerance; without it we would need to eat unfeasibly high quantities of other mineral-rich foods.

One year earlier a different conclusion had been reached by Angela Epstein in the Daily Mail 30 November 2004 (p.44). She said that 'in recent years scientific evidence

The Milkman

had linked different types of milk to a variety of health scares; in the week of the article, Swedish researchers had declared that drinking more than one glass of milk a day could double the risk of ovarian cancer.' The news, she declared, could further contribute to the drop in the nations milk consumption which was thought to be declining at the rate of two per cent a year. The opposing views of the two articles make for confusing reading.

Mrs Beeton's remarks were prophetic when she said 'The quality and wholesomeness of milk depends greatly on the food and home of the animal'. She also commented 'from no other substance, solid or fluid, can so great a number of distinct kinds of aliment be prepared as from milk all of them wholesome and some medicinal'. Her test for milk was 'Dip a bright steel knitting needle into the milk. If the milk drops off slowly, it is pure, but if it runs off quickly leaving the needle bright, it has been adulterated with water.' I wonder what she would think of skimmed milk. We might be forgiven for concluding that consumption of organic milk from a known source, as Mrs Beeton's comments, would be a suitable recommendation. In a later edition of her books it says that 'the best popular test for adulteration by water is by means of a small instrument called a lactometer'. There are notes on milk for young children 'for it is their best and most natural food'.

The Food Standards Agency refers to the benefits of milk, pointing out that it contains vitamins and minerals such as calcium. It doesn't cause tooth decay – unlike the poten-

The Milkman

tial of some fruit juices. As a warning it adds 'watch out for flavoured milks, milk shakes, condensed milk and milk-based energy or malt drinks, these tend to contain added sugar, which is bad for the teeth; milk and dairy products are an important part of a child's diet and a good source of energy and protein.'

The Pot of Tea

Mrs Beeton's comments on making tea show another world from the present use of tea bags. She admits 'there is very little art in making good tea; if the water is boiling and there is no sparing of the fragrant leaf, the beverage will almost invariably be good. However this depends on a teaspoonful for each person, warming the pot with boiling water, leave for 2-3 minutes, then pour away. Then put in the tea pour in a half to three quarters of a pint of freshly boiled water, close the lid and let it stand for 5-10 minutes'. It would be better to think that we would make time to go through this procedure; it needs some good taste buds to appreciate it fully. Green tea is noted by Mrs Beeton; she warns that strong green tea disagrees with some persons and should never be under-taken by them.

The Pot of Tea

Over 150 years later the Consumers Association's magazine 'Which' on line, February 2006, gave their view on making tea and what makes the perfect cuppa. Comparing the two there is not much difference between them but 'Which' now admits the use of tea bags. While Mrs Beeton lets her tea stand for 5-10 minutes 'Which' allows 5 minutes; 'stir the tea and add a teaspoon of tea for the pot, when ready put a small amount of milk in a cup before pouring'. 'Which' goes on to recommend the traditional bone china tea set but admits that we now tend to use mugs. In its full report on tea it states it contains flavanoids that may help to protect from heart disease.

―――――――

The magazine 'Healthy' of September/October 2004 (p.54) referred to green tea through nutrition consultant Ian Marber. He pointed out that the Chinese have been drinking tea for over 4000 years to promote health. In recent decades scientists have begun scrutinising this ancient brew. Its health benefits are owed to a high polyphenol content, with the antioxidant effect 20 times more potent than vitamin E, in most other tea.

―――――――

The Sunday Times 'Style' (p.51) 12 November 2006; Jennifer Harper-Deacon confirmed the benefits of green tea and

The Pot of Tea

its powerful antioxidants; she says it helps to restrict the
build-up of blood cholesterol, lower blood sugar levels,
reduce high blood pressure and suppress the ageing
process; also that a cup contains 30mg of caffeine compared with 40mg in black tea; she cautions that the
decaffeinated green tea process may affect health benefits.

The Coffee Bean

Mrs Beeton would have been horrified at the words 'instant coffee'. She says 'to have coffee in perfection it should be roasted and ground just before it is used.' She noted that the introduction of coffee into this country is comparatively of recent date. It was first introduced in England in the early 19th century. The coffee tree was a native of Abyssinia and coffee had been cultivated in that country from time immemorial. She goes on to say that of the various kinds of coffee the Arabian is the best, chiefly grown in the districts of Aden and Mocha. She makes mention of the importance of roasting, then a separate business with considerable skill needed.

No mention of caffeine content is made, and coming back to reality, the FSA seem more concerned with this ingredient and its effects; also the determination of its level per serving. They refer to caffeine as a known stimulant of the central nervous system occurring naturally in coffee and tea. Following a survey they warn pregnant women about the wide range of caffeine levels in coffee.

Fruit Juices

While most of the fruits we now buy are described or used in Mrs Beeton's recipes, their use as a base for juices and juice drinks is not recorded; orangeade and lemonade are featured however, each with plenty of sugar. There was little commercial exploitation of this market. Mrs Beeton makes reference to popular American drinks maintaining they are remarkably palatable; they include pineapple water, straw-berry water and currant water, all with a high content of sugar. Her comments on children's food seem equally to apply to drinks when she says that 'it should be more nour-ishing than stimulating'. Perhaps another way of saying that colourful fruit drinks are bound to catch a child's eye.

Suppliers of fruit juices and drinks are in a very profitable field. Their marketing is colourful and we can be bowled over by the wording. We also need to look closely at the sugar contents and juice percentage. Visits to supermarkets showed these examples:

Fruit Juices

	Sugar (100ml)	Juice
Sainsburys Cranberry Juice	11.5g	10%
Pomegreat (RJA Foods)	26.5g	37%
Cranberry & Pomegrate (Ocean Spray)	11.5g	19%
Grove Fresh Organic Apple & Mango	11.2g	100%
Grape, Raspberry & Blueberries	9.8g	20%
Tesco Pomegranate Juice Drink	12.2g	100% (30% pomegranate)
Grape, Raspberry and Blueberry (Cape)	9.8g	20%
Pomegreat 100	12.6g	70% pomegranate + juice to give 100%
Adez Blackcurrant & Raspberry	4.6g	20%
Tesco Blueberry drink	11.3g	18%
Sirco apple & blueberry juice drink	11.4g	21.5%
Somerfield Pomegranate fruit juice drink	11.3g	30% pomegranate + juices to give 50%
Sainsburys pure red and white grape juice	15.4g	100%
Fairtrade pure orange juice	10.5g	100%

Fruit juice drinks, as distinct from juices, are cheaper but not necessarily of good value. They may contain a limited amount of juice but with a high sugar content. The conse-

Fruit Juices

quences of too much sugar is discussed separately. Fruit drinks with less than 2g of sugar per 100g can be taken as low with above 10g as high.

Sometimes the drinks have an 'unsweetened' label; they can still add up to around 15 grams of sugar per 100ml to bring a juice up to a standard level of sweetness; it then sells better.

The total nutritional information needs to be well-considered. Where the percentage of juice is less than 50% it is likely the main content is water. This applies to over half of the list. There may be an additive, sweetener, preservative or thickener included.

———⟫•◦•⟪———

Juice contents vary as will be seen; the description of a fruit drink may lead us to think that the juice is the major constituent; it turns out that other fruits are included; we are being mislead.

The use of concentrate which is arrived at by compressing the fruit and freezing the juice ready for shipping by sea or air to a destination for the addition of water, is often noted. Transport costs are saved. Pure juice however should be used to describe juices that are made from one particular fruit, with no added ingredients.

The chilled juice category is fresh squeezed juices not treated in any other way. They are sold refrigerated with a

Fruit Juices

short life – maybe two to three days. Other juices are also sold chilled but have been pasteurised or heat treated after squeezing to kill off the yeasts in the juice to give a longer shelf life of 3 weeks to 3 months.

I sought the advice of the FSA on juices and they replied on 24 July 2007: 'The sugars found naturally in whole fruit are less likely to cause tooth decay, because the sugar is contained within the structure of the fruit. But when fruit is juiced or blended the sugar is released. Once released, these sugars can damage teeth, especially if fruit juice is drunk frequently. When you are choosing fruit juice, remember to check the labels carefully to make sure you are buying 100% fruit juice and there is no added sugar. Also watch out for 'juice drinks', which contain as little as 5% fruit juice and contain a lot of sugar. You may find that the drinks which have less than 10% fruit juice, are actually 'juice drinks' – which we recommend you watch out for. The fruit juices with 100% fruit juice would have less added sugars in them, which would be better to blend with fruit. Juice drinks have added sugar (in addition to natural sugars from fruits), so these are not so good for your health when compared to 100% fruit juices'.

Fruit Juices

The ingredients lists are revealing; they should be read as important as the nutritional information. Within these lists generally varied additions occur: Citric Acid, Aronia juice, puree, glucose & fructose syrup, stabiliser (pectin) colour (lutein), dicalcium phosphate, nicotinamide and pantothenic acid. As remarked elsewhere we really need a degree in chemistry to appreciate these benefits, should they be so.

*"You need eight glasses a day and one
magnifying glass to read the info."*

8

Healthier Hearts

Mrs Beeton is famous for her BOHM; for the most part the recipes. To her, management of the household, and her readers well being, were equally important, one topic relating to the other. She included a chapter headed 'the Doctor'.

Earlier editions refer to 'Palpitation of the Heart' advising that it does not necessarily mean heart disease and is more likely due to indigestion, and flatulence.

When briefly referring to 'Heart Disease' Mrs Beeton cautions 'if there is any suspicion of its existence, if there is a shortness of breath, pain over the heart or running down the left arm, any labouring or irregularity in the heart's action, medical advice should be sought and carried out'.

A disease of the heart or circulatory system is now affecting an increasing number of us. Scientific research indicates that the risk may relate to several causes: smoking, not exercising, high blood pressure, high cholesterol levels, being overweight, not limiting alcohol, and diabetes. We may need to adjust our life style to fight them. The ban by the government on smoking in certain areas, in July 2007, has highlighted one of the causes.

⟶•⟵

We receive much information relating to heart disease and its prevention; hopefully these extracts relating to a beneficial diet will give a picture to the reader:

The magazine 'Healthy' April 2004 (p.65), said that nearly all heart disease is preventable; 'we should eat lots of fruit, vegetables, cereals and fish, less red meat and saturated fat; this should halve the risk of cardiovascular disease; stick to government guidelines in drinking alcohol to reap the antioxidant and blood thinning benefits of alcohol.'

The Somerfield supermarket magazine of January 2005 (p.43), paid attention to the heart. It declared it is important to eat a diet high in fruit, vegetables and fibre and low in salt and fat. Sensible drinking is noted to be within the published guidelines. It also maintained that cholesterol levels in the blood are raised by foods high in saturated fat including sausages, butter, hard cheese, cream and cakes; we should

eat fewer foods containing hydrogenated fats like some biscuits, fast food, pastry, margarine and spreads.

Daily Mail 1 February 2005 (p.48); Jenny Hope 'Britons
drinking three cups of black tea a day will keep heart attacks
at bay'. Her research showed that those drinking four cups
a day picked up optimum benefits.

The Daily Telegraph gave a full page spread on 28
November 2006 (p.20), heading 'Spice up your life and save
your heart'. In another article in the same paper Professor
Roger Corder had referred to the beneficial effects of red
wine and he now referred to antioxidants called procyanides
that help protect against the build up of fatty deposits in the
arteries. Apart from wine he said that there are many alternative sources of procyanides such as apples, cranberries,
pomegranates, raspberries, berry fruits and cinnamon.

The Times 20 February 2007 (p.27); Nigel Hawkes
Health Editor forecasts 'A generation faces years of misery
due to heart disease'. He pronounced that a leading heart
charity (Heart UK) had declared that Britain faced a health
and pensions crisis as baby boomers fall prey to heart disease and strokes; also that high cholesterol levels – the
single most important cause of the disease – can be con-
trolled by a healthy diet and lifestyle.

Daily Mail 15 May 2007 (p.21); Jenny Hope, Medical
Correspondent, 'Mediterranean diet halves risk of lung disease;' while this diet referred primarily to the lungs she also
remarked that 'Doctors have already claimed the Mediterranean diet – high in fruit, vegetables, fish and 'healthy' fats,
such as those in olive oil, while low in red meat and dairy

products, can improve heart health.' She commented again on the Mediterranean diet on 23 May 2007, when she related that 'Experts drawing up guidelines for the National Institute for Health and Clinical Excellence said lifestyle changes are as important as drugs in preventing another heart attack and that patients will be told to follow a Mediterranean diet'.

———————

Following visits to Spain I have commented in Appendix A on aspects of this diet; it is said to be of help in the prevention of other diseases as well.

From the extracts we can focus on fruit and vegetables, with consideration of lifestyle changes. A reader may observe that having read extracts from the articles I have related, I should be very aware of the importance of what they said. However in February 2007, I was the victim of a near fatal heart attack and in March underwent bypass surgery. I thought that since my wife died, I had satisfied risk factors relating to blood pressure and cholesterol level.

I was treated in two hospitals and both had a post operative nutrition and dieting service.

The first hospital prescribes action to achieve a heart friendly diet:

    Reduce total fat intake
    Reduce salt intake
    Try to eat more oily fish – aim for 2-3 times per week
    Aim for five portions of fruit and vegetables each day

Try to include more fibre in your diet
Increase exercise
Reach and maintain a healthy weight
Moderate alcohol intake.

The second hospital advises under the heading 'Your cholesterol lowering diet'. Its aim is to give general principles about what changes are necessary to the diet to help lower the cholesterol level. It supports all the aims of the first hospital; in addition it maintains that stress needs to be reduced; also to cut down on sugar because it contains only empty calories with no other nutrients. This assists an overweight problem.

Having maintained that I had satisfied all the risk factors I felt a little reassured when both hospitals commented on the likelihood of an inherited condition particularly relating to high blood cholesterol. My father died from a heart attack when in his mid fifties. Medical reactions to it and subsequent treatment were then less advanced so that I have felt rather fortunate, or was it a case of mis-management?

Perhaps a warning to readers to investigate their family history.

9

Cancer Care

The terror of the word 'cancer' to mid Victorians may be summed up by Mrs Beeton's words 'The very name of this disease is fraught with so much significance, and the diagnosis is a matter of so much doubt to the lay mind, that the subject becomes out of the scope of this work. In the case of any tumour being discovered, medical advice should be taken at once.'

While cancer has this brief reference in earlier editions of the BOHM there were many more diseases receiving treatment as she records: smallpox – the discovery of vaccination; scarlet fever – most cases recover in a fortnight; typhoid fever – caused chiefly by the contamination of drinking water with sewage; typhus fever, cholera – common in unfavourable hygienic conditions. While these diseases are now under limited control we record today over 40 different cancers affecting our bodies.

Michael Van Straten and Barbara Griggs are authors of a book published 17 years ago entitled 'Super Foods'. It records foods under the heading of preventative nutrition, with general advice to enhance the body's natural defences against cancer and other diseases. Their advice has stood the test of time: they refer to risk factors such as 'a poor diet; heavy smoking; exposure at work to toxic chemicals; heavy alcohol consumption; obesity; family history of cancer; long periods of bad eating habits; high levels of stress; unhappiness or frustration'.

They listed five four-star super foods: apricots, beetroot, cabbages, carrots, garlic. Other super foods were listed: all the citrus fruits, berries and currants, apples, apricots, bananas, all the vegetables, seeds and nuts, garlic, dried fruits, drinks – fruit and vegetable.

Today additional emphasis can be given to that in the book. More than one or two drinks of alcohol a day can increase chances of developing several types of cancer. Red wine seems better endowed with cancer preventative polyphenols than other drinks. Avoid excess salt. Eat less sugar and sugar containing foods. Keep fat intake low.

Headlines and writings in the press relating to the disease are informative and well meaning. However when a book or an aspect of the disease is reviewed there must be a natural tendency towards the eye catching headline, they then need interpretation through the reading of the whole article.

Our concerns over the possibility of catching this disease are born out in press headlines. Please see the references at the end of this chapter.

'Hold back the clock. How plants can tackle the diseases of old age'.

'A quarter of a million lives could be saved each year through dietary changes alone.'

'8 ways to fight prostate cancer.'

'Cancer risk toxin detected in food.'

'How brazil nuts can beat cancer.'

'Cancer hazard in packed salad.'

'Cancer checks on all spices.'

Avoiding the disease is subject to continual research. There will be more advice, with the reader quite likely to end up confused. The effects of any guidance may vary between individuals. A diet today heavy with processed foods, may contribute towards the accumulation of toxic chemicals relating to the disease.

An analysis of present day research on foods to buy, to fight this disease, may be summarised:

Vegetables – 21 different ones altogether: especially broccoli, sprouts and cauliflower.

Dried fruits generally: especially apricots and prunes.

Grains: barley, brown rice, buckwheat, millet, wholewheat and wheatgerm.

Pulses, lentils, chickpeas, all the beans.

Seeds, nuts: almonds (part of a Mediterranean diet), hazelnuts, pumpkin, sesame, sunflower seeds.

Herbs: there are eight recommended out of the many on the market, garlic gets a star rating.

Other foods: extra virgin olive oil and yogurt, quark and sauerkraut.

Drinks: fermented fruit and vegetable juices, especially beetroot, cabbage, carrot and potato.

⟶•○•⟵

A reminder that the European Commission estimates a quarter of a million lives could be saved each year through dietary changes alone.

References

Superfoods – Michael Van Straten and Barbara Griggs published by Dorling Kindersley Limited, London

Hold back the clock – Dr. James Duke, Daily Mail 12.4.04 (p.38)

The European Commission estimates a quarter million lives could be saved each year through dietary changes alone – 'Healthy' March/April '04 (p.51)

8 Ways to fight prostate cancer – Adapted by Anne Shooter from Understand, Prevent and Overcome Prostate Cancer by Professor Jane Plant CBE, Daily Mail 13.7.04 (p.45)

How Brazil nuts can beat cancer – Tim Utton & Robin Yapp, Daily Mail 10.9.04 (p.5)

Cancer hazard in packed salad – Zoe Catchpole, Daily Mail 11.9.04 (p.15)

Cancer checks ordered on all spices in the new food dye alert – Valerie Elliot and Nicola Woolcock The Times 3.5.05 (p.1)

Good diet helps in cancer treatment – Barbara Lantin Daily Telegraph 10.7.06 (p.23).

10

Overweight or Obese

Mrs Beeton remarks on obesity: 'to overload a child with food is the surest way of making him puny or small, and after middle life if people get heavier it is because they accumulate stores of fat, which is the reverse of an advantage'.

A century and a half later the Food Standards Agency declares that it means that someone has put on weight to the point that it could seriously endanger their health. This is caused by a combination of eating too many calories and not doing enough physical activity. It also says that being overweight or obese increases the risk of developing heart disease, Type 2 diabetes, high blood pressure and osteoarthritis; we should follow a balanced diet by not eating more calories than we need.

Mrs Beeton focused, mainly, on her cooking and recipes; not necessarily considering obesity as one leading to other diseases. Health campaigners were also absorbed by unsanitary living conditions. The contagious diseases of her time were likely to be smallpox, scarlet fever, consumption, cholera, typhoid, typhus and pneumonia.

——➤•◦•◄——

Daily Mail 14 September 2004 (p.33); Sean Poulter, Consumer Affairs Correspondent: 'Piled high, the daily dose of obese Britain.' He said that Britons were eating themselves into an early grave; the findings paint a picture of a nation fighting a losing battle against obesity with serious long term implications for health.

These figures, he revealed, were based on a study of thousands of dieters across the country.

Daily Mail 30 November 2004 (p.40); Charlotte Dovey: 'walking can prevent obesity by lowering cholesterol and help to strengthen the heart.' She emphasizes that the type of walking is the key and quotes the head of medical information at the British Heart Foundation who said 'You know its worth it when you feel warm and slightly puffed'.

The Daily Telegraph 3 December 2004 (p.22), Judith Woods: 'an estimated quarter of men are obese.' One of the problems, she said, is in the attitudes of men and their desire to be a macho man because calorie counting and low fat do not have the same image to impress. 'Low carb' has a rather macho ring to it. She in turn quotes Amanda Johnson of the British Dietetic Association who says 'we would be worried about any kind of diet that excludes whole food groups; we promote messages about things men can incorporate into their lifestyle – reduced portion sizes, more fresh fruit and vegetables, fewer Friday night pints;' Judith Woods indicates further that manufacturers are vying with each other to introduce 'low carb' versions of products effectively creating a multi million pound industry in months; she maintains that there are a lot of products appearing on supermarket shelves which are 'low carb' but contain the same number of calories as the original product.

The Times 26 February 2005 (p5); Sam Lister, health correspondent: 'more than eight million are now dangerously obese, a quarter of all adults are dangerously overweight following a 75% increase in obesity in the last decade'.

The Sunday Times 15 July 2007 (p.6); Jon Ungoed-Thomas: 'one of the biggest studies into the eating habits of Britain's poorest families has gone against conventional wisdom by finding their nutritional intake is similar to the rest of the country.' It was the result of a £5m study by the FSA which looked at the eating habits of 3,500 people; it found that the nutritional value of the food eaten by the poorest 15% in society was little different from the average. Obesity was at a similar level among the poor as it was in the general population. The article said the findings would now be circulated to relevant government departments and agencies.

The FSA uses the Body Mass Index (BMI) to say whether we are overweight or obese. The BMI is calculated by taking our weight in kilogrammes (kg) divided by our height in metres (m) squared, so that a man who weights 85kg and is 1.75m tall will have a BMI of 28. A BMI over 25 is defined as overweight whilst over 30 is obese. It is worth noting that it is the distribution of fat that can cause health complications rather than body weight.

One recommendation the FSA do make is to cut down on children's sugary drinks, such as fizzy drinks and squashes. They are then less likely to put on weight. They also recommend physical activity without defining it; follow a balanced diet and consider also the additional weight on the body's joints; possibly leading to aches and pains, particularly in later life. This alone may have a crucial impact on health, raising the risk of catching a disease.

Before we interpret all the foregoing under the headings perhaps we should consider whether we are prone to overweight because it is in our genes? In an article in The Times 2 June 2007 (p.38), Mark Henderson Science Editor discussed our genetic future: he referred to the fact that in April (2007) it had been announced that the first common gene that has shown reliably to contribute to obesity, had been discovered.

As with many other published findings resulting from scientific discoveries we will not receive benefit from the discovery until it is fully authorised.

A book 'French Women don't get fat;'* was brought out

by French born and bred writer Mirielle Guilaiano in 2005. She brings years of experience and practical advice to women's lives and says 'French women eat with their heads, and they do not leave the table feeling stuffed or guilty'. Her comments may fall on sympathetic ears as 'Banish the diet book. You need what French women have: a balanced diet and time tested relationship to food and life'.

————

Obesity is a chronic condition and hard to ignore. Weight loss programmes do not guarantee fitness because most are based on a temporary loss of weight, instead of a long term behavioural programme. We are advised that a waist measurement of greater than 36 inches may be a high-risk profile for heart disease.

Millions would like to lose weight; obesity is a disorder which occupies the minds of governments. This relates particularly to the welfare of children – our future generation – who are attracted by increasing numbers of fast food outlets. Additionally convenience stores are multiplying.

It is a paradox that there are many starving people in the world and yet there are those more prosperous trying to eat less.

* Published by Chatto & Windus in 2005

11

Living Longer

Mrs Beeton was caring about living longer. There are 80 pages devoted to illnesses and treatments. They commence with a mother's responsibilities and her influence over children, ending with convalescence. When she refers to keeping well she remarks 'health of body and mind is a blessing of inestimable value, and, as the greatest of all earthly means of happiness; the efforts of all wise persons should be directed towards its attainment'.

———◦———

There are over 2,000 recipes in the BOHM. Mrs Beeton adjudges avoiding indigestion as very important; she declares 'we might just as well expect a locomotive without plenty of fuel to function as expect a human body to perform its daily labour without a due supply of suitable food, properly chewed, swallowed and digested.'

When referring to old people she adds 'they must either be careful of their diet or soundly chastised for their neglect, complete mastication of the food is vitally important to health and long life.'

All her words are full of good advice and must have been greatly appreciated by her readers. We will note that much of what she put into words still applies today.

However before the mid-Victorian era a connection had been found between being overweight and illness; it could not have received the publicity it deserved; it is fair to say that some of Mrs Beeton's recipes induced obesity.

One hundred and fifty years after Mrs Beeton's death life expectancy has risen and is rising. This statement has to be qualified for the maintenance of health varies between the developed countries and those poverty stricken ones where food is short.

Many books and articles have been written on this subject; apart from our desire to live longer, information under this heading will relate also to diseases in general. Passages from the media help us to interpret the research; we must hope we are not misguided if it is ongoing or incomplete. Media writers may well have their pieces edited and be subject to marketing, with the addition of headlines and subheadings. An editor may have different ideas as to what his readers want. Should we feel that qualified writers have done enough investigating to give proper advice there are certain foods that are beneficial. Lives may be at stake if their advice is not correctly given, hence many conditions or qualifications. We may be confused by recipes and cooking hints that come after; the many and varying methods are often difficult to follow for the newcomer or non cook.

———————

To get some idea of a consensus from writers as to the foods giving the greatest benefits I have abstracted articles at random. It is safe to assume that they are seen by a greater readership than some more official notifications.

Daily Mail 15 June 2004 (p.47): 'How to add years to your life in just one day,' it pointed at the average British woman. It was based on our increasingly unhealthy modern lifestyles; it purported to show how chances of living longer could be boosted. It listed activities that could be undertaken every half hour or hourly or thereabouts. It started with the exhortation to eat breakfast at 7.00 a.m., finishing the day at 11.30 p.m., advising not to stay up too late. Food recommendations included 11.00 a.m. two cups of tea, 1p.m. fish for lunch particularly omega 3 fatty acids, with three portions a week. 4 p.m. snacking on fruit, and to eat five portions of fruit and vegetables a day. At 7.30 p.m. it said that having a drink should be beneficial because people who drink in moderation have a longer life expectancy than those who are teetotal. An interesting listing is feasting on broccoli at 8 p.m. because of its plentiful antioxidants; also live yoghurt. It further states that another good source of antioxidants is dark chocolate containing 70 per cent cocoa or more, with the provision of no more than two squares a day.

In summer 2004, The Sunday Times through their 'Style' section of the paper introduced essential anti-ageing foods explaining how you can drop excess calories and pounds without suffering hunger pangs if you follow the principles of high fibre, low glycemic index, eating the right fats.

The top anti-ageing foods are listed as:

Brazil nuts because they are bursting with selenium

Salmon – rich in omega 3

Cherries

Lean steak – an excellent provider of protein

Sweet potatoes – one of the richest providers of vitamin E

Soya milk giving potential skin benefits

Mineral water benefits, from certain brands

Strawberries – essential nutrients with skin benefits

Shell fish giving skin benefits

Nori and other seaweeds with sources of iodine, again with skin benefits

The Times 4 September 2004 (p.17): 'can you eat your way to a longer life?' The article noted that there were clear indications that some foods can help prevent wear and tear. As with other findings fruit and vegetables came out well along with those that have dark pigments such as prunes, blueberries and blackberries. Dark-pigmented vegetables as kale and spinach were advocated. Of the 26 fruit and vegetables put forward it was said that they all decrease the signs and illnesses of ageing.

Daily Mail 17 December 2004 (p.21): a reporter advised a 'simple diet that could add six years to your life;' according to researchers in the Netherlands consuming the following foods regularly could cut the risk of heart disease by 76 per cent:

Wine – one small glass daily 32%

Fish – one serving four times a week 14%

Dark chocolate – 3.5oz a day 21%

Fruit and vegetables – 14 oz a day 21%

Garlic – 2.7g a day 25%

Almonds – a handful a day 12.5%

Daily Mail 30 December 2004 (p.36): Angela Epstein ' How to live to 100!'. Two celebrities Sophia Loren and Yoko Ono are pictured. The article posed the question ' could we all be living to the age of 100 with the right food and lifestyle'. It gave examples of locations in China, Italy, Japan, Greece and Pakistan and listed food eaten in each:

China: Sweet potatoes and pumpkins, tomatoes and peppers, amaranth, hemp, corn, brown rice and herbs.

Italy: Fruit and vegetables, almonds, fish – anchovies and sardines, lean meat, wine, malt drinks.

Japan: Sweet potatoes, soya, seaweed, freshly caught fish, whole grain and noodles, meat with the fat cut off, green tea.

Greece: Extra virgin olive oil, artichokes, tomatoes.

Pakistan: Apricots, fruits and nuts, vegetables, root vegetables, chapattis, beans and pulses.

The passage indicated that all life expectancy in parts of these countries is greater than our own.

Daily Mail 18 January 2005 (p.40): Angela Epstein 'Your Perfect Health Day' it is an interesting exercise to compare it with that article on '15 June 2004' – detailed earlier under this heading, 'How to add years to your life in just one day'. Again it seems it was addressed more to those British women with time on their hands and no children to look after. Comparing it with '15 June' breakfast is at 7.40 a.m. and both recommend a bowl of porridge. The snack is at 10.30 a.m. with tea not mentioned. Lunch does not note fish but recommends a high protein meal. The afternoon at 3.30 p.m. gets round to a tea, expressly limiting any caffeine content. An hour later a pot of yoghurt is noted. A drink is beneficial at either 7 p.m. or 7.30pm. when both are recommending red wine. Dinner is at 8 p.m. but a large meal is to be avoided because it puts the digestive system into overdrive affecting sleep. The two articles have differing advice but the essentials are comparable.

An abstract of articles makes interesting reading for similar results are being made known beyond the years 2004-5. Broccoli, tomatoes, oranges and onions are listed three times as a top choice; spinach, kale, cabbage, Brussels sprouts, beetroot, blueberries, are twice cited. Others named are sweet potatoes, pumpkin, cherries, raspberries, strawberries, cranberries, blackberries, kiwi fruit, white and red grapes, plums, prunes and pink grapefruit.

Fish rates almost as much importance as fruit and vegetables, in particular those with omega-3 oils; wild salmon, seaweeds and shellfish.

Other favourable mentions are garlic and dark chocolate

(three times), red peppers and oats (twice); seeds and nuts, in particular brazils, almonds, walnuts, flaxseed; beans generally, yoghurt (live), soy, soya milk, lean steak and turkey, honey, sage, raisins, liquorice and avocado (once). Of the drinks tap water is very much accepted as vital to our well-being usually in the shape of 2 litres a day; mineral water also gets a mention but only certain brands. Within limits of consumption wine is approved for its health benefits. Caffeine free teas, noting green tea, are twice named alongside black tea.

Readers may agree that there are many qualifying factors attached to the conclusions, for foods may vary in quality; they may go beyond their 'best before' date when ready to be eaten. Those foods contained in packaged and processed foods may not have the same nutritional benefit as those bought from local markets.

━━━━━➤➣○◆━━━━━

Food cooked at home to a recipe containing a balanced diet selected from the previous articles, should give the greatest benefit. Many vegetables may be eaten raw particularly in summer salads; or they can be lightly steamed to give maximum nutritional benefit to bones and skin, and boosting immunity. This chapter relates very much to those comments under my headings Cancer Care, Healthier hearts Obesity and overweight, Salt, fat and sugar.

━━━━━➤➣○◆━━━━━

The foods noted and abstracted contain antioxidants. There is a 'boxing' match going on in the cells of our bodies; the free radicals – the polluters associated with ageing – are trying to get in; the anti-oxidants will be fighting to stop them; it is important to feed well with these to achieve that longer life.

"Life painting."

12

The Big Challenge of the Supermarkets

It is a challenge to keep up with the trading operations of the supermarkets. They are part of a changing lifestyle for millions of customers who stop by them. I was drawn to them to manage, or possibly mismanage, my changed living experience.

I have visited different supermarket stores in this country and Spain, not only to buy but to see their layouts and marketing methods; to try to understand them. We know they must persuade everyone in the store to get more than they need; the contest begins.

At the entrance we are usually welcomed by a blast of warm air. We may well feel relaxed and reflect that it is an agreeable place. We may however be in a transition period, not thinking too purposefully. In most stores there is a neutral area; we become accustomed to the multiplicity of colour and sound that greets us; some stores do sell papers and minor items here but we are not meant to dwell; we move quickly on to a mainly windowless area where the supermarket would like us to focus attention on our purchases. We must not be distracted by what is going on inside by looking outside. Lack of windows gives the store more wall space.

Most often we see firstly the fruit and vegetables section, which is always colourful. It sets us into a mood for buying, moving on to the rest of the store.

We usually need bread, meat and milk. These goods are found at the back or near to the back; we then have to walk past hundreds of items so positioned to catch our eye. Being essential, a store would not place them near the front in order to try to coerce us to stay in the store longer. Bread baked on the premises has diverting baking smells wafting through aisles to attract us.

As we walk up and down the aisles we slow down as we turn round to the next. Very often there are strategically placed 'great' offers at the ends. The temptation to buy at this point is quite strong. We have passed through themed lanes, trying hard to pick out the best value. It must be assumed that items are carefully placed; at eye level we are buying what the store want us to buy. On the lowest shelves there may well be items that appeal to children. In a less prominent position we will find the alcohol and drinks section; this has to be discovered by the customer for it is not in the aisle seen when entering the store; presumably that would not give the right image.

Supermarkets aim to make a visit enjoyable right through the store. Assistants, if available, are trained to be polite and helpful. If they are asked about the nutrition percentages and ingredients of their goods however, they have a woeful lack of knowledge.

———————

We come eventually to the checkouts with their adjacent sweets and fancies. We very often have to wait; if there are children queuing there is more temptation to add to a basket. A cashier's job must be one of the more soul destroying around and no wonder the turnover is high. There are set piece words to customers with a persuasion to make us aware of the company's reward or points card scheme. The information on our cards can be used for further marketing of their goods. Not to have one seems to bring forth a slight sigh of astonishment. Presumably the cashiers are being filmed on cameras, as are customers. There will also be supervisors carefully making sure that they do not have to open up another cash point until really necessary.

The majority of us are now matched to the supermarkets for our household management and possible mismanagement. The choices available are growing.

Local stores cannot have a cross section of our total needs; there are those customers who are turning to exotic foreign foods, now being imported by the supermarkets in increasing amounts. Many of us are busy people with limitations on time. This could lead to an allegiance to a distance for stores visited; what we eat in terms of variety.

The Guardian 16 March 2004 (p21) George Monbiot: 'The Fruits of Poverty'. He remarked that the superstores have used their buying power to force the world's farmers to compete directly with each other. The British farmer is selling his fruit for less than the cost of production to compete with overseas, where labour is cheap and farms huge. By forcing down the prices of the goods they buy, the superstores encourage regressive conditions, which could be described as a form of slavery. As the superstores capture the market, they shut down all our choices: about where we shop, what we buy, who we work for. As he says, this is what monopolies seek to do.

Information from the Liberal Democratic Party in March 2004, was reviewed by Simon Crompton, The Times, 13 March (p2 Body & Soul news). It said that we spend £15 billion on packaging every year and that supermarkets need to do much more to reduce it. It costs us money and obliges us to spend time sorting it for the recycling bins.

The Daily Telegraph 11 July 2005 (p17) Judith Woods: 'Food Miles that leave a bad taste:' before reaching our supermarket shelves much of our fruit and vegetables has travelled thousands of miles, resulting in a significant reduction of vital nutrients. Examples on the shelves of a supermarket might contain sugar snap peas from Guatemala, kiwi fruit from Chile, pre-packaged salad pota- toes from Israel, broccoli from Spain.' She noted that lots of research showed that for fresh fruit and vegetables, nutri- ents like vitamin C begin to deplete almost as soon as something has been picked and taken out of the ground.

A further item on the theme of food travelling to our plates from afar appeared in the Daily Mail, 13 September 2005 (p47), Angela Dowden investigated. She referred to it as the crazy world of far flung food. Additional travels included orange juice from Brazil, strawberries from Amer- ica, Braeburn apples from New Zealand, carrots from Spain. mangetout from Kenya. After each instance of travel she suggested alternatives so that we could buy British.

The Daily Telegraph 24 January 2007, under 'News', fea- tured a banner headline 'Supermarkets fuelling binge drinking' They were selling alcohol at below cost price and using alcohol as a loss leader to tempt customers away from local stores. The write-up also dwelt on the plight of British farmers who are forced to sell to supermarkets at artificially low prices: it said that small shops such as bakers and butch- ers were being forced out of business by the supermarket stranglehold. There seems to be no end to the domination of our purchasing through competing supermarkets. On 24 January 2007 (p6) the Daily Mail's Consumer Affairs Corre- spondent, Sean Poulter, highlighted additional figures from the Competition Commission. These indicated that more than 12,000 independent food stores have been lost in the past six years. The figures included 9,600 convenience outlets and 2,830 butchers, bakers, greengrocers and fish-mongers. The article cited a town, Bicester, in Oxfordshire, which now had six Tesco outlets in a market town of 30,000 people. Before the supermarket's arrival there were six butchers, three fishmongers, three ironmongers and two gro-cers. Only two of these shops have survived. Store tricks included selling basic items such as bread at below cost price in a bid to lure customers away from small stores.

Joanna Blytheman has examined the hidden costs of the growing concentration of the power held over us by the supermarkets. They claim that their innovations have broad-ened the palate by introducing new tastes and flavours. Her investigations concluded that they are mainly selling the same standard components continuously re-assembled and re-marketed in a multiplicity of forms. A supplier observed to her that U.K. supermarkets would stop selling fresh unprocessed food entirely, if they thought they could get away with it; it is just too much hassle. In the case of fish caught in Scotland they are routinely sent to distribution cen-tres in England, before being transported back to Scottish stores. 'Fresh' fruit and vegetables may have been har-vested prematurely to stop them deteriorating during transportation and on the shelf. She gives instances of how supermarkets justify these policies relating to spinach, leeks, celery, herbs, strawberries, lettuce, mangos, melons, turnips, plums, apples, carrots, potatoes and bread, with many more illustrations.

The above brief comments were extracted by the Daily

Mail of 26 April 2004, from her book 'Shopper'. 'The Shock-
ing Power of British Supermarkets'.

Official investigations into the growing power over us of the
supermarkets, seem to occur now and again without a result
that greatly limits their activities. However, early in 2007 the
Competition Commission's interim findings were reported in
The Daily Telegraph Business News for 24 January 2007
(p.32). Richard Fletcher reported on figures published at the
start of the second stage of an industry enquiry now
described as 'emerging thinking'. He noted that six years
ago the Competition Commission concluded that while the
grocery market 'was broadly competitive' they had concerns
about the balance of power between suppliers and retailers.
He noted also that six years later Tesco and others still per-
sist in many of the practices that sparked concern before.
On page 34 of the same Telegraph supplement he also said
the inquiry would now focus on issues including examining
whether local monopolies existed. They would look at
Tescos or other supermarkets domination to see if they are
in such a strong position either nationally or locally, that no
other retailer can compete effectively.

I have found information on food components confusing.
There has been an uncertain feeling of being lead astray.
Buying processed foods and looking at the ingredients and
nutritional information almost requires a knowledge of
chemistry. Recommended daily guidelines for sugar, salt and

fat may be exceeded in one meal. Then there is the colour-ful labelling carefully designed by marketing teams; goods quite often claim to have health benefits. It gives the impression that most labels are games to make us buy, whatever the make up of the food. This despite the fact that labels on food must not be misleading when related to guidelines. During visits I became somewhat bewitched by the colour and the clever marketing. The use of words like authentic, naturally better, natures way, traditional, country style, value and economy ranges, mean very little when looked at closely. Time is necessary to understand their intentions. When it comes to the word 'processed' it could be said to relate to much of the food that we buy – more than we think. On 12 February 2004, the FSA issued criteria and guidance for the Use of Terms: fresh, pure, natural, traditional, original, authentic, home made and farmhouse. The survey covered 220 samples and of these 88 (40%) were considered by the participating public analysts not to comply.

I have referred to the FSA for information on labelling although the European Union is the ultimate arbiter. This very fact may make any action against manufacturers concerning inaccurate information on a label, too time consuming to combat. The supermarkets have their own brands. These are invariably cheaper than the branded suppliers; they often have limited detail of the constituents.

Having visited Spain and sampled their foods in various restaurants I was intrigued by Sainsburys 'Mediterranean style' processed foods. They included one: 'chicken breast with wild rocket and lemon dressing'. I imagined this was a processed meal remindful of Spain. It was a 400 gram pack containing in all 38.8g fat, 4.0g salt and 11.2g sugars.

It said that the 'citrus, peppery accents of wild rocket and lemon infuse these tender chicken breasts, complemented by a crunchy garlic pangrietta topping' I bought it on the spot. When I looked at the ingredients listed in order of weight, I noted: Chicken breast (55%), Cherry Tomato, Double cream, Vegetarian Mozzarella cheese, Wild Rocket (4%), Extra Virgin Olive Oil, Butter, Water, Breadcrumb (Wheat Flour, Yeast, Sugar, Wheat Gluten, Salt, Emulsifier: Mono and DiGlycerides of Fatty Acids; Dextrose, Flour Improver: L-Ascorbic Acid), Modified Maize Starch, Salt, Concentrated Lemon Juice, Emulsifier: Mono & DiGlycerides of Fatty Acids (with Dextrose): Garlic Puree, Dextrose, Sugar, Parsley, Antioxidant: Potassium Citrate; Stabiliser: Sodium Triphosphate; Black pepper.

———————

I have listed all the ingredients but did not understand much of what was set down. I was aware however of the FSA guidelines that men should eat no more than 95g of fat per day and women 70g; salt is recommended at about 6g for men and women. Half a pack was not enough for one meal and I ate the whole pack (425g). I was eating a half of the fat recommendation and two thirds of salt for the one day. I was in the dark about the benefits of most of the other ingredients and bemused by the marketing words crunchy garlic pangrietta topping; I could not taste this flavour in the meal.

The contents are a challenge for the customer; while there are the legal requirements to list nutritional information a separate ingredients list may qualify it. There will also be the marketing disguises and certainly there should be more ethical and honest labelling. The meal was purchased in February 2005; on 22 March I read in the Daily Mail (p.40) an article by Felicity Lawrence exposing 'the grim reality of chicken production'. It was enough to put anyone off buying chicken, let alone the tender chicken breast that I had bought. It also said that chicken is the most common source of infection, relating to salmonella poisoning.

Further observations on Mediterranean style eating were featured in The Daily Telegraph 8 April 2005 (p.7): Celia Hall, Medical Editor. She said that a study of 74,000 older men and women, including 10,000 British participants concluded that a Mediterranean diet will give people an extra year of life. Increased life expectancy was linked to a diet high in vegetables, pulses, lentils, fruit, cereals and fish. The healthiest diet was low in saturated animal fats but high in the unsaturated, like olive oil. It was also low in dairy products and meat but included a modest amount of alcohol – usually wine. The article also went on to say that the plant based diet was popular with older people in Spain and Greece. Recent visits to Spain have further illustrated the difference in eating habits between our two countries. We might well conclude that we could live longer in Spain. I have outlined later my experiences from visiting there.

The Times 28 April 2007 (p43), Thomas Catan: of the top 11 restaurants in the world chosen by Britain's 'Restaurant' magazine four are in Spain. He said that Spaniards spend more per head on eating than other Europeans and that the best restaurant in the world, as chosen by an international panel of 650 food critics, was in the Costa Brava – for the second consecutive year.

Daily Mail 15 May 2007 (p.21), Jenny Hope, Medical Correspondent: 'a diet rich in Mediterranean foods can halve the risk of developing serious lung disease', say researchers. Also that 'doctors have already claimed the Mediterranean diet – high in fruit, vegetables, fish and 'healthy' fats such as those in olive oil, while low in red meat and dairy products – can improve heart health and help stave off cancer.'

———⟫─○─⟪———

The Daily Telegraph 21 February 2007 (p28): Iain Hollingshead described an eight hour stay at a 100,000 sq. ft. Tesco store. After breakfast in the store he noted the services and goods. They provided for an instore travel agency and travel insurance, all the prerequisites for kitting out a starter home, buying an overseas home, jewellery, watch repairs, pharmacy, personal finance, car insurance, opticians, funeral tokens and many more services; they would even allow us to purchase everything we need to eat to live. Multi-cultural diverse Britain was also catered for with one aisle containing huge vats of Asian cooking oil.

The Daily Telegraph 22 January 2007 (p.65): Josephine Moulds visualised the future of supermarket growth. It was Tescos largest regeneration scheme yet. It comprised 960 homes, council offices, a health care facility with 40,000 sq. ft of small shops; a large Tesco store had been approved. An observer may well conjecture on the profitability and tenancy of the small shops if Tescos remain as their landlords.

13

Farmers Markets

The Sunday Times 8 April 2007 (p.7) Jonathan Ungoed-Thomas and Claire Newell: 'Farmers Markets sell supermarket foods.' They pointed out that these markets were supposed to put integrity back in the food chain. The markets are only supposed to stock local produce. They said also that under the rules of The National Farmers' Retail & Markets Association (FARMA), produce must be typically sourced from within a 30 mile radius, although this can be extended up to 100 miles for markets in London. A principal producer, or someone directly involved in production, should be on the stall. FARMA itself amplified the definition of a farmers' market saying that it is a market in which farmers, growers or producers from a defined local area are present, in person, to sell their own produce, direct to the public. All products sold should have been grown, reared, caught, brewed, pickled, baked, smoked or processed by the stall-holder. The two reporters said that a Sunday Times investigation has found evidence that farmers' markets are not all they seem; they related results of their investigations. They had, for example, discovered spinach from Portugal and Spain – produced by another supermarket supplier – being sold at a market in Kent. They also found evidence that even legitimate stallholders are 'topping up' their locally grown produce with vegetables bought from Britain's whole-sale markets.

From their joint investigations The Sunday Times had concocted what they called the 'Farm bluffers guide': 'Roll your vegetables around in the mud to give them an authen-tic farmer's market look and you mark up your prices accordingly.

Tear off labels saying Spanish or grown in Argentina and replace, giving the name of a quaint sounding farm, or that it is locally grown. Give yourself and your (Polish) stall-holders names like Tess and Gabriel. Ditch your normal weekend clothes and get wellies, a smock and a cap or scarf on your head. Get a CD of farmyard noises and make sure it plays in the background for added credibility. Have a rant about modern pesticides. Make it clear to customers that you only use the countryside's natural fertilizers and you will win their undying loyalty.'

The above guide could be said to be amusing if it were not for the health implications.

We should consider questioning stallholders as to the

origins of their goods; we should benefit by purchasing their fresh produce.

A closing statement was made by a representative of FARMA who said the best way to safeguard the integrity of the markets was for them all to be properly certified and that FARMA was considering new procedures that would certify stallholders. They have also said that there are over 500 Farmers' markets in the country with only half genuine FARMA certified Farmers' markets.

14

Conclusion

I feel anyone trying to benefit from a new diet related lifestyle must end up confused. Perhaps this word would be a better one as a heading than 'conclusion'.

Until my wife died my visits to a small local supermarket were usually limited to buying a few necessities. Supermarkets are criticized but will continue to expand. They will carry on fighting the planning authorities and objections to their growth. They have overwhelming asset backed finance and need to satisfy the demands of their shareholders who are always seeking more profitable returns. Their expansion has taken place in a relatively short space of time; in the lifetimes of many of us. Their need to increase their capacity will also grow as the social mix of the country changes; increasing the demand for native and exotic foods. In Mrs Beeton's day perhaps we may compare this change with the Industrial

Revolution and birth of the railways; this was the time when there was movement from the rural way of life to the cities.

As the supermarkets influence us we may well at the same time be receiving advice from nutritionists, dieticians, new scientific research; also the media in its many forms, medical advice and other specialists. We may be confused by their words; advice we receive one day can be different from the next. We need also to take into account however the fact that researchers may well have done years of costly work before coming to a conclusion on their findings. From their point of view they might veer towards a positive or controversial finding that may satisfy their sponsors and get them publicity. A particular part of the media may have a vested interest in publicising a story and making it run and run. Every day there is a new scare to consider; there are claims and counter claims publicising a story and making it continue. A university or academic institute which is funding research could want a beneficial report for publication, perhaps creating one before completion of the research. Powerful public relations companies may be hired; there is also the danger that the media, in any form, may not publish a full story because they are seeking the eye catching headline that attracts their readers: the actual article becomes a précis of the full research.

Buying from supermarkets is very convenient for those busy people short of time; and they may well not see a scare story relating to supermarkets, or their goods; or equally a beneficial one. Perhaps what we do not know we will not worry about and are none the worse for it. There are also the marketing teams confusing us, as they may do, with their misleading words, use of colour, artistic packaging design, and photographs. We might say we could do without them so that we could form our own conclusions, but we may not buy so much; supermarkets could be duller places. They might well persuade us we are entering a dreamland that itself relaxes us so that we buy more. Their marketing is geared purely to getting the goods sold. The amount of data food makers provide for consumers is up to them. The marketing personnel have a massive brief as most food labels will testify. It is confusing for customers and it is meant to be; it may be difficult to make a correct choice. This becomes important when considering the implications of a disease which may benefit, or not, from a particular food or drink. Supermarkets may find that eventually the European Union will step in with new legislation to curb their many misleading or unsubstantiated statements about the health benefits of food and drink. It could assist our judgements as to what we should buy.

In whichever country we are staying or living we may find differing interpretations of food benefits. Statistics indicate that longevity does vary as between countries and diet is very often given as the reason.

It is perhaps unfair to compare with our own, the lifestyle of Mrs Beeton and the middle class Victorians. Living in a house then, managing it without electrical aids surely involved more physical exercise particularly for women in the lower social classes without servants; indicating that they should have had some health benefits. The average age at death was, however, much lower than the present; health had not benefited by the tremendous advances in medical science and treatment of diseases.

We might observe that there may have been a much higher incidence of obesity in Victorian times in view of an interpretation of some of Mrs Beeton's recipes. Mrs Beeton was buying, in effect, home produce from the few shops available or growing it in a garden or allotment without the use of pesticides. Their food would have reached the dining table without having to travel by sea and air. The food should have been the better for it.

Society tends to take deterioration with ageing that happens, and is acceptable. Fortunately new research is continuing and is challenging long held beliefs. When we stop learning and are inactive we may become old. The ageing process itself does not bring this about.

We should consider the fact that many adults who participate in active pastimes are fitter than many inactive youngsters. Combine inaction with a lowly diet and we have a faulty lifestyle. This is epitomised by pictures of care homes with rows of old people in easy chairs.

Readers may qualify as old because of a government statistic which says that men and women are entitled to benefit in their early sixties. It is unimaginable that we are adjudged to be old by numbers. On this basis there are many in their 90's who may be 25 years past their 'sell by' date. The truth is that they still have much to offer a society; this is based on activity and diet. They show up many who are much younger. Unfortunately many of us have little idea how to feed ourselves.

To brighten up our day, a meal including food not recommended – a cream cake or a sugary drink – cannot mean that an occasional one including these is out of place; there must be some diversions in life. If I followed everything that I had read or learnt, then eating could be an uninteresting part of life. Perhaps some of my conclusions will lead readers to consider a change to their diet and lifestyle.

I have tried to convince readers that diet does play an important part in longevity and I hope that what I have written may generate greater interest. Should this be so then I will have achieved my objective.

⎯⎯⎯⎯⎯≫·∘·≪⎯⎯⎯⎯⎯

"Doesn't the future look confused?"

Appendix A

Mediterranean Diet

I have been fortunate to visit Madrid and its surrounding towns and villages over the last fifteen years, staying with my daughter. This has enabled me to enjoy both Spanish home cooking and eating out in restaurants. In Madrid there are daily food markets with fresh fruits, vegetables and freshly butchered meat carcasses; sea food is a favourite and Spanish consumption is stated as second only to Japan. Stallholders have a good knowledge of what they are selling; quality ingredients are the key with seasonal freshness.

Rice, citrus fruits, almonds, dates, aubergines, apricots, peaches, quinces are cultivated. A Spanish kitchen may contain olives, olive oil, rice, almonds, seeds, garlic, saffron, ham, cured and raw sausages with choice of cheeses. We may well have a satisfying experience in eating. Spaniards have a head start to reach our five servings of fruit and vegetables each day. When eating out we inevitably receive good service in the restaurants with well cooked food; usually the waiters are only too pleased to discuss their menu and wine list.

Local food markets are facing increasing competition from the supermarkets. Those visited – apart from the smaller local and specialist ones – were bigger than our own with wider aisles. There are massive counters for fish, fresh fruit, vegetables and cheeses. Also there appears to be less imports and a smaller area of frozen food consequently reducing freight or air miles.

The Spanish seem to eat and drink all day and part of the night. A siesta after lunch helps but they certainly do enjoy their food; we could well change our own diet by following their principles. It would help to reduce cholesterol levels, one of the risks relating to heart disease.

———————

After one of my visits I came across the following comments about living in a Mediterranean country. Dr. Anne Nugent, a nutrition scientist with the British Nutrition Foundation declared in 'Healthy' March/April 2004, 'The Mediterranean lifestyle promotes a longer, healthier and youthful life. This is due to all-year-round fresh fruits and vegetables, outdoor living and less stress levels. Also a diet with vitamin-E rich extra virgin oil as a staple helps protect the brain against age related deterioration.'

The Times 22 September 2004 Nigel Hawkes remarked: 'Elderly people who eat a Mediterranean diet, drink moderately, keep active and avoid smoking can live significantly longer than those who don't. The Mediterranean diet was high in fruit, vegetables, nuts, seeds and grain, relatively low in meat and meat products and high in olive oil rather than fats. A Mediterranean diet rich in plant foods in combination with non-smoking, moderate alcohol consumption and at least 30 minutes of physical activity per day is associated with significantly lower mortality rate even in old age'.

I have noted under 'Healthier hearts' another reference to the Mediterranean diet. Daily Mail 9 October 2007 (p.38): Angela Epstein drew up a list of hints on escaping the ageing process at various ages. She maintained that 'those who followed the Mediterranean diet lived longer. A study led by the University of Athens examined 74,000 healthy adults from nine countries.'

I wonder how the many thousands of British visitors and those now living in Spain would agree with what has been said. My own experience is based on eating in the central area of Spain. On the coast many Spanish menus could be influenced by tourists who are not evident in the capital. A Spanish diet and lifestyle may allow readers who have visited Spain to compare with their own.

"Remember, a Mediterranean diet isn't just for holidays, it's for life."

Appendix B

Definitions for the Baffled

Added Value Products (premium products) Something has been done to the product to add value to the consumer. It may provide a health benefit.

Additives Added to food in small amounts to perform a technological function such as adding colour, flavour or texture. 'E' numbers are accepted by the E.U. If not then approved by an expert panel before they can be used in food. Some may be added for cosmetic reasons or to disguise cheap ingredients.

Antioxidants

Substances produced by the body or drawn from the diet that neutralise destructive compounds that might cause degenerative diseases. Some vitamins may play a role in fighting harmful free radicals in our bodies.

Best before date

Shows the consumer the period when the food is in its best condition if kept according to the manufacturers instructions. These are usually found on tins, frozen foods and packets.

Bio

Most yoghurt labelled with the word 'Bio' claim to contain 'live' bacteria.

Calcium

Needed for the formation of bones and teeth. Vitamin D helps calcium to be absorbed by the body. Foods containing calcium are milk, cheese, white flour and green vegetables.

Calories

The calorific value of a food is

arrived at by adding the energy given by the constituents. For an adult person of normal weight it could be somewhere in the neighbourhood of 1,600 calories per day rising to about 4,000 calories for hard continuous labour. The figures on the label is the total figure contained including starches and sugars.

Carbohydrates (carbon plus water)

Foods include bread, pasta, breakfast cereals, potatoes and rice. Digestible carbohydrates give us energy within our diet. Nutriional information may say that the carbohydrate is 50g 'of which sugar' is 10g. The starch remaining is therefore 40g.

Dietary fibre

Name used to describe the soluble or insoluble carbohydrates found in foods of plant origins. It is found in wholemeal bread, high fibre breakfast cereals and fruit and vegetables.

Display until

Used by some shops to help with stock control and are instructions to shop staff, not shoppers.

Emulsifiers

Common additives in processed foods which include mayonnaise, low fat spreads, salad dressings.

Fat

Energy-producing power weight for weight more than any other food. Rich source of energy made up of fatty acids and glycerine.

Saturated. Animal and dairy produce. Source of cholesterol that circulates in blood and made in the liver. Has the effect of raising the cholesterol level.

Unsaturated. Vegetable oils from soya bean, olives, maize and sunflower and other seeds and nuts. Also marine oils from fish (e.g. cod liver oil). Both omega-3 and omega-6 fatty acids are polyunsaturated fats.

Free from

A food may claim to be 'free from artificial preservatives' but it may contain other ingredients that have a preserving effect (such as salt).

Free radicals

Highly reactive fragments of a molecule that result from air pollution, radiation, cigarette smoke, or incomplete breakdown of fats and protein in the body. A free radical can attack fats in the body, release harmful substances into surrounding cells and rupture their membranes. Increased production may result in the furring of coronary arteries.

Irradiation

Food may be exposed to high energy radiation to reduce or destroy unwanted micro organisms. However it may affect the wholesomeness of some foods by preventing the sprouting of vegetables and ripening of certain fruits.

Labelling

This is governed by an E.U. Directive and nutrition labelling is required per 100g with an option for an average serving

Processed food packets contain the standardised nutritional information with seven nutrients listed as Energy, Protein, Carbohydrates – of which sugars, fat – also listing saturates, fibre and sodium.

Minerals

Health benefits are very often deemed to be obtainable from calcium, selenium, potassium, zinc, phosphorus, magnesium, iron; no doubt others as research advances.

Prebiotics   Plant sugars which nurture the growth of healthy or 'good' bacteria in the gut.

Preservatives   A processed food with a long shelf life may include preservatives, unless another way of keeping it has been used as canning, drying or freezing.

Probiotics   The high density population of friendly bacteria which aid our digestion.

Protein   The main constituents of poultry, eggs, cheese, lentils, fish and meat for example. It is important for body growth and repair, providing amino acids (chains of building blocks) and therefore energy. One gram equals four calories.

Sodium   The part of salt that can lead to high blood pressure. 1g of sodium is 2.5g of salt. No added salt means that the manufacturers have not added any salt or sodium when made.

Stabilisers   These are substances which help to retain the consistency, texture and appearance of processed foods.

Sugars   Added sugars. These sweeten food products and include corn syrup, honey, sucrose and glucose etc.

No added Sugar. The food has not had sugar added to it as an ingredient. It may contain ingredients (such as fruit) that have a naturally high or an artificial sweetener which may have been used to give the food a sweet taste.
Unsweetened. This may mean that no sugar or sweetener has been added to the food to make it taste sweet. It doesn't mean that the food contains no sugar.

Trans Fats   Occur naturally in small amounts in dairy products and meat. Formed artificially when manufactured, hydrogenated fat turns the fat solid and also extends the shelf

	life. Said to clog arteries whilst having no nutritional benefit.
'Use by' date	Self explanatory and using it after the date shown could put health at risk. Necessary to act on instructions on the pack. Usually found on food that may go off more quickly such as meat, fish, salads.
Vitamins	They are a group of organic compounds which are essential for growth and nutrition. They are required in small quantities in the diet because they cannot be synthesised by the body. They are measured in milligrams or micrograms. Brief definitions of some of the vitamins follow and they are extracts from various publications.

Vitamins	Function	Source/Examples
A	Helps body's immune system for fighting infection. Necessary for normal growth and for healthy eyes and skin.	Animal foods Vegetables

Vitamins	Function	Source/Examples
B1 – Thiamine	Metabolising carbohydrates.	Wholemeal bread Breakfast cereals potatoes, pork, brown rice.
B2 – Riboflavin	Healthy eyes and skin.	Potatoes, fish, eggs, milk, cheese
B6 – Pyridoxine	Healthy nervous system.	Fish, carrots, pulses, beef and poultry
B12 – Cobalamine	Healthy nervous system.	Oily fish, meat, liver, milk, eggs
C	Healthy immune system. Necessary for healthy function of cells. Increases production of infection-fighting white blood cells.	Vegetables and fruit (particularly citrus)
D	Strong bones and teeth	Fish liver oil, cheese, milk, eggs, vegetables

Vitamins	Function	Source/Examples
E	Antioxidant against free radicals.	Vegetables nuts including walnuts, almonds, seeds
K	Normal blood clotting.	Vegetables Lean meat

The recommendation for suitable intake of vitamins could well centre on fresh fruit and vegetables, dairy products and nuts, cereals and fish. This is coupled with a reduction of processed and pre cooked foods.

Understanding nutritional information

Energy

There are two units of energy expressed on nutritional information.

The calorific value of a food is arrived at by adding the energy given by the constituents and is usually expressed in kilocalories (kcal) or kilojoules (kJ):

kcal = 1000 cal

kJ = 1000 J

1 kcal = 4.18 kJ

For an adult person of normal weight calories needed could be somewhere in the neighbourhood of 1600 calories per day rising to about 4,000 calories for hard continuous labour.

Weight/Mass
28.35 gram = 1oz

453.6 gram = 1 lb

1 kilogram = 2.2 lb = 1000 gram

1 gram = 1000 milligram (mg)

1 mg = 1000 microgams (µg)

Volume/capacity
1 fluid ounce (fl oz) = 28.4 millilitre (ml)

1 pint = 20 fl oz = 568 ml

1 litre = 1.76 pt = 35.12 fl oz

Appendix C

Selected References

Pre Mrs Beeton
New System of Domestic Cookery By a 'Lady'
John Murray, London, 1821
Modern Cookery in all its branches, Eliza Acton
Longman, Brown, Green and Longmans, London, 1849

Books relating to the Life of Mrs Beeton
(dates of publication not always stated)
Mrs Beeton's Dictionary of Everyday Cookery,
S O Beeton, London, 1865

Mrs Beeton's Household Management

Ward Lock & Co, London

Mrs Beeton's Book of Household Management

Ward Lock & Co, London (Three editions)

The Book of Household Management, Mrs Isabella Beeton

Ward Lock & Tyler, London

Beeton's Every-Day Cookery and Housekeeping Book

Ward Lock & Co, London

Mrs Beeton's Every-day Cookery (several editions)

Ward Lock & Co, London

Mrs Beeton's Cookery Book (two editions)

Ward Lock & Co, London

Mrs Beeton's Family Cookery

Ward Lock & Co, London

Biographies of Mrs Beeton

Mrs Beeton and her husband, Nancy Spain,

London, 1948

Mr and Mrs Beeton

H. Montgomery Hyde, London, 1951

The Short Life & Long Times of Mrs Beeton

Kathryn Hughes, London 2005

Extracts from Mrs Beeton's Books

Essential Beeton – Isabella Beeton

Summersdale Publishers Ltd, Chichester, 2004

The best of Mrs Beeton's Household Tips

Weidenfeld & Nicholson, London, 2006

The best of Mrs Beeton's Every-day Cooking

Weidenfeld & Nicholson, London, 2006

The best of Mrs Beeton's Easy Entertaining

Weidenfeld & Nicholson, London 2007

Books relating to diet and nutrition

How to keep your cholesterol in check

Dr. Robert Povey, London 1997

Essential Fats

Dr. Michael Colgan, Canada, 1998

Complete Nutrition

Dr. Michael Sharon, London, 2001

Eat Right for Your Type

Dr. Peter J.D'Adamo, London 2001

Eat Well, stay young

michel/montignac, London, 2001

Nutrition and Health

Gerald Wiseman, London, 2002

Body Foods for Life
Jane Clarke, London 2002
Age Power
Vermilion (Ebury Press), London, 2002
Dr. Ali's Nutrition Bible
Dr. Mosaraf Ali, London, 2003
Eat Drink & Be Healthy
Walter C. Willett, America, 2003
Nutrients A-Z
Dr. Michael Sharon, London, 2004
Not on the Label
Felicity Lawrence, London, 2004
'L' is for Labels
Amanda Ursell, London, 2004
The Food Doctor Everyday Diet
Ian Marber, London, 2005
Top 100 Immunity Boosters
Charlotte Haigh, London, 2005
Never Say Diet
Drew Fobbester, London, 2005
Everything you need to know about dieting
David Charles, UK, 2005
What are you really eating
Amanda Ursell, London, 2005
French Women Don't Get Fat
Mireille Guiliano, London, 2005
Stay Fit after Fifty
Rozalind Graham, London, 2006

Super Foods
Virgin Books, London, 2006
Your diet questions answered
Quadrille Publishing Ltd, London, 2006
Wonder Foods
Natalie Savona, London, 2006
Superjuice
Michael van Straten, London, 2007
The Truth about Food
Jill Fullerton-Smith, London, 2007
You are what you eat
Catrina Morris, London, 2007
101 Facts you should know about your food
John Farndon, Cambridge, 2007
1001 Ways to stay young naturally
Susannah Marriott, London, 2007
Read the Label
Richard Emerson, London, 2007
How to be a Healthy Weight
Phillipa Pigache, London, 2007

Index

NOTES

NOTES